At Issue

Should College Athletes Be Paid?

Other Books in the At Issue Series:

At Issue

Should College Athletes Be Paid?

Geoff Griffin, Book Editor

GREENHAVEN PRESS

An imprint of Thomson Gale, a part of The Thomson Corporation

Detroit • New York • San Francisco • New Haven, Conn. • Waterville, Maine • London

Christine Nasso, *Publisher*
Elizabeth Des Chenes, *Managing Editor*

© 2008 The Gale Group.

Star logo is a trademark and Gale and Greenhaven Press are registered trademarks used herein under license.

For more information, contact:
Greenhaven Press
27500 Drake Rd.
Farmington Hills, MI 48331-3535
Or you can visit our Internet site at http://www.gale.com

LIBRARY OF CONGRESS CATALOGING-IN-PUBLICATION DATA

Should College Athletes Be Paid? / Geoff Griffin, book editor.
    p. cm. -- (At issue)
 Includes bibliographical references and index.
 ISBN-13: 978-0-7377-3789-9 (hardcover)
 ISBN-13: 978-0-7377-3790-5 (pbk.)
   1. College sports--Economic aspects--United States. 2. College athletes--United States--Economic conditions. I. Griffin, Geoff.
   GV350.S36 2008
   796.04'30973--dc22

                                                        2007028832

ISBN-10: 0-7377-3789-1 (hardcover)
ISBN-10: 0-7377-3790-5 (pbk.)

Printed in the United States of America
10 9 8 7 6 5 4 3 2 1

Contents

Introduction

The issue of what incentives or rewards college athletes should receive beyond their basic scholarship is hotly debated on both sides, even as a revolution is taking place within the National Collegiate Athletic Association (NCAA) which will help college athletes by placing a greater degree of responsibility for their education on the institutions that claim to be educating them. On January 10, 2005, the NCAA voted to require that its member institutions make a yearly Academic Progress Report (APR) on their performance to keep athletes eligible and help them progress toward graduation. Athletic teams at those schools which fail to produce adequate results can be punished when members of the team fail classes or leave school.

This is a significant departure from the way the college sports system has operated for decades. Over the years, one of the arguments against athletic scholarships was that athletic departments have had little incentive to promote the "student" half of the student-athlete model. Athletic departments, and more specifically coaches, have control over rewarding scholarships that are renewed on a year-to-year basis. In the past, a coach was more likely to look at how the athlete played on the field when making the renewal decision rather than rewarding classroom performance. After all, the coach had no specific responsibility to make sure the players graduated and he or she was likely to be judged on wins rather than graduates. The coaches and athletic departments did have an interest in making sure that athletes met the minimum academic requirements to be eligible to compete, and if a star player dropped out it might hurt the team competitively; however, it was more likely that the player dropping out would be the one harmed in the long run rather than the team, coach, or athletic department.

For the first time in its history, the NCAA now has a system where someone other than the athlete can be subjected to penalties when that athlete becomes ineligible or drops out. Under APR, a student-athlete can earn two points each year for his or her team—one for remaining eligible and one for remaining in school or graduating. Students are expected to be 40 percent of the way to a degree after their second year, 60 percent after their third year, and 80 percent after their fourth year.

APR is determined by taking the number of points actually earned by a team, dividing that number by the number of points possible for that team and converting that score to a scale of 1,000. (APR = (points earned / points possible) x 1,000) For example, if a basketball team has 10 scholarship athletes, those 10 athletes can earn a possible 20 points. If nine of those athletes stay eligible and remain in school, but one becomes ineligible and drops out, the team would have a total of 18 points. The APR for the team would be 900. (18/20 = 0.9 x 1,000 = 900).

The NCAA has set 925 as the required score for any given team, a figure it maintains translates to a graduation rate of 60 percent. Teams that score below that number can be penalized in a variety of ways, including losing up to 10 percent of their scholarships. Teams that score below 900 on a consistent basis (a 45 percent graduation rate) can become ineligible for postseason play and suffer other penalties. The penalties apply only to a specific team in a specific sport, not the university athletic department as a whole.

In 2006 and the spring of 2007 the NCAA handed out penalties and warning letters to a relatively small number of teams, but the number of teams penalized could grow exponentially in the spring of 2008. So far, the NCAA has allowed teams to take waivers for "squad-size adjustments" when a program has a statistically small number of scholarship athletes. The waiver will no longer be available for most programs in 2008, and the number of teams that might end up falling below the 925 score is staggering. If the squad-size adjustment waivers had not been available in 2007, 44 percent of men's basketball teams, 40 percent of football teams and 35 percent of baseball teams would have fallen below the 925 mark.

The NCAA is so concerned with the numbers for men's basketball, which along with football is one of the two main revenue producing sports for colleges and the NCAA, that on May 29, 2007, it formed a group to look at the men's basketball problem and make recommendations to the NCAA Division I Board of Directors by the end of 2008.

"Nothing will be off the table," NCAA President Myles Brand said in an Associated Press report about the formation of the group. "We need to work together to . . . ensure basketball student-athletes are as successful in the classroom as they are on the court."

While the APR system represents a new direction for college sports, it is just one of many issues relating to the rights of student-athletes and responsibilities of the institutions they attend. Viewpoints on a variety of these topics are addressed in *At Issue: Should College Athletes Be Paid?*

1

Paying College Athletes Makes Economic Sense

Rodney D. Fort

Rodney D. Fort is a professor of economics at Washington State University. He is author of the book Sports Economics *and co-author with James Quirk of the books* Pay Dirt *and* Hard Ball. *His articles also appear in numerous academic journals.*

Many people have an aversion to paying college athletes for their services, but an examination of various principles of economics show that paying athletes makes sense and would make the college sports system more efficient in the way it distributes money. Players would receive more of the revenues they produce while pay would be cut for administrators and other employees in athletic departments. Many of the arguments that are made against compensating college athletes do not make sense when viewed from an economic perspective.

If competition ruled the market for college players, rather than colleges working through the National Collegiate Athletic Association (NCAA), there would be no amateur requirement, no recruiting restrictions, and players would be free to move between teams subject to any contractual obligations with their current college team. The absence of an amateur requirement would mean that players would be free to negotiate whatever compensation arrangement was mutually agreeable to them and their university. For some players, the current scholarship arrangement might suffice. For others, it would not.

Few topics evoke the same level of gut-reaction disapproval than play for pay, that is, paying salaries to college players in addition to, or instead of, full tuition grants. Economists have commented on this issue for nearly 20 years ... and it is a hot topic even today. We will ... address a few of the arguments against doing so. ...

If you think that college players should not be paid more than their current level of compensation, you are in the majority. Surveys have revealed that nearly 64 percent of those polled were against play for pay. ... Let's look at the four main arguments against play for pay and make of them what we can from an economic perspective.

Where Will the Money Come From?

One argument against play for pay is that athletic departments barely break even in the first place. ... A few make money, mostly on football and men's basketball, but not the vast majority. So, where will the money to pay players come from?

This argument is confused for two reasons. First, it really is not the case that athletic departments break even in any meaningful sense of that term. Universities allow athletic departments to keep all excess revenues on an updated basis during any given budget period. Thus, a department whose costs do not rise over budgeted amounts, but whose revenues are higher than expected, will appear to break even because they are allowed to spend the excess. So there can be plenty of revenue to be rearranged.

The second confusion is that one does not need to worry where the money will come from because it is already there. Under the current amateur requirements, players generated their MRP [marginal revenue product or the amount of revenue a player creates], and it is then spent elsewhere in the athletic department rather than on players. Remember, just because players do not receive their MRP does not mean that it goes away. It is spent in other areas of the athletic department.

Won't Non-Revenue-Generating Sports Be Harmed, Especially Women's Sports?

The argument that play for pay would harm non-revenue-generating sports recognizes that the money that would go to players under play for pay would come from other parts of the athletic department. Setting the argument in this way pits play for pay against allocations to other sports in the athletic department. Opponents of play for pay forecast dire consequences for low-revenue sports. A common fear is that the ability of the high-revenue sports, typically football and men's basketball, to support the rest would be reduced. This fear is especially worrisome to those supporting gender equity if the high-revenue sports are supporting women's sports.

If athletic directors cut a sport, or reduce spending on a sport, they are cutting their department's net revenue position.

The clue to the confusion here is in the way the argument sets revenue sports against so-called non-revenue-generating sports, but omits all of the other lines in the athletic department budget from consideration. The notable omissions are administrative salaries, coaches' salaries, recruiting, and facilities. If the world changed to play for pay, where would play for pay funds come from? The answer, of course, is from those areas, that currently, are overpaid relative to their actual MRP. Suppose it is other men's sports that are currently overpaid. This would mean that prior to play for pay, the athletic director was investing in those sports at a higher rate than their [performance] would support. The same goes for women's sports, with one additional feature. Federal and state laws require spending to ensure gender equity, therefore the athletic director would spend on women's sports until that margin is met. The athletic director would have no reason to wastefully overspend on either men's or women's sports.

If athletic directors cut a sport, or reduce spending on a sport, they are cutting their department's net revenue position. If sports are cut or reduced, the success of the department falls below the best level that athletic department can obtain. Athletic directors might wish they could rearrange money in this fashion, and they may use such threats to try to sway others against play for pay, but that option simply is not believable. At least it is not believable as long as athletic directors care about the bottom line of their department.

Won't Wealthy Athletic Departments Just Buy All the Best Players?

In a play-for-pay world, some argue that wealthy schools would buy the best players. The idea behind this argument is that rich, successful athletic departments would be able to outbid their competitors for athletic talent and would buy up all the top-quality players. The result, according to this argument, would be competitive imbalance that would ruin college sports for fans. Fans of all but the top teams would lose interest, and their teams would suffer even further revenue declines. Ultimately, those colleges might simply drop out of Division I-A. Fans at all but a few colleges would be as bad off as they possibly could be.

[D]ifferent people are paid different amounts in all employment markets. College sports would be no different.

There is a single response to this misunderstanding ... players already go to the athletic departments where they are most highly valued. This means that the richer, stronger schools already get the bulk of the most talented players. Play for pay will not change the distribution of talent because talent already is distributed in a way that generates the best bottom line for athletic departments. Coupled with our answer to the last question, play for pay would just make coaches and administrators in athletic departments poorer, but talent would still be distributed in approximately the same way.

Won't Different Players in Different Sports Be Paid Differently? Especially Women?

Another argument against play for pay rests on an inescapable observation about markets and pay: People get paid different amounts. The issue raised by this question is the usual one of the fairness of such an outcome. How can differential payment to athletes be fair? Also, in an era where departments are striving for gender equity, how can it be fair to pay those in revenue-producing sports, primarily men, more than those playing non-revenue-generating sports, primarily women?

In a play-for-pay world, there would be differential pay.... We would expect that quarterbacks would be paid more than second-string offensive linemen....

The argument against differential pay is one of fairness. However, in debates on differential pay, nobody argues that people should not be paid at all. Besides, even if you want a *fairer* way of paying players, then you still want them to be paid. In short, different people are paid different amounts in all employment markets. College sports would be no different. Again, coaches and administrators would see their pay reduced under play for pay, but it is hard to imagine that any athlete can be worse off if all are getting paid (albeit different amounts).

Enough Already! They're Already Given a Free Education

The final argument against play for pay centers on the fact that scholarship athletes are given a subsidized chance to earn the future income returns and quality of life that go along with a college education. Some judge that to be more than enough. In addition, a select few are given the chance to pursue the mammoth incomes earned by professional athletes. However, this argument has two shortcomings.

The first shortcoming is that some (I repeat, *some*) athletes do not value the educational component of their time spent in college very highly. This irritates many people who hold a college education in high regard. However, the preferences of athletes cannot be invalidated just because some observers wish they had a greater appreciation for their educational opportunity. In fact, as with all things, the value of this type of payment is an entirely subjective exercise. Since it is value received that matters when discussing compensation, only the athlete can know the value of the scholarship to them. This means that, for some athletes, compensation in the form of educational opportunity is worth little.

A second shortcoming to the argument that an education is sufficient compensation is that some athletes contribute more revenue to the athletic department than the value of their scholarship. . . .

Arguing that athletes get paid enough is now a value judgment, and any person is free to pass such judgments. But consider this: Do you think that *you* should get paid *your MRP* at *your* job, even though you might be willing to work for less if you had to?

2

Pay to Play: Should College Athletes Be Paid?

Krikor Meshefejian

Krikor Meshefejian is a senior editor for the Journal of the Business Law Society.

There are several persuasive arguments as to why college athletes should be paid, but those arguments ultimately fail because the first duty of a university is to educate, not to hire entertainers. Despite the failings of the current system, paying athletes runs contrary to the primary function of educational institutions.

Does it make sense for an academic institution to run a multimillion dollar entertainment business, which is what college football and college basketball have become? Does it make sense for these institutions to pay the student-athletes who participate in these football and basketball programs?

The reality is that college sports programs, namely the "big name" programs such as football and basketball programs at marquee schools, are businesses that stand to make a large amount of money for their respective schools. According to an article in the *Harvard Journal on Legislation*, "[i]n the past twelve years, the amount of money generated by these two sports has increased nearly 300%, such that they now fund almost all other sports programs." The student-athletes who participate in these programs are part of the reason why these schools stand to make such handsome profits: through ticket

Krikor Meshefejian, "Pay to Play: Should College Athletes Be Paid?" *The Journal of the Business Law Society*, March 23, 2005. Reproduced by permission.

sales, endorsement deals, broadcasting deals, and jersey sales (although player names cannot be represented on jerseys), among other things.

Mark Murphy, Director of Athletics at Northwestern University, who participated in an ESPN [sports television network] debate on the topic of paying student-athletes, argues that these athletes currently receive scholarships, whose value, in some instances, totals close to $200,000 over four years. He stated that all student-athletes have made similar commitments to the schools, and that football and basketball players should not be treated any different than other athletes, who participate in sports that are not as popular and lucrative. Paying athletes anything beyond a scholarship, argues Murphy, would cause problems, particularly from a gender equity standpoint. What Murphy seems to be referring to when he says "gender equity" is Title IX federal regulations, which cut off federal funding of colleges if those colleges discriminate on the basis of sex. Paying male student athletes more than female student-athletes could possibly be construed as discrimination.

Arguments for Payment

However, others argue that these athletes are producing revenues not only for the schools, which gives these students scholarships, but also for shoe companies, television networks, and the conference in which these schools belong. Moreover, the equity problem could obviously be solved if all collegiate athletes get paid the same base salary for their participation.

There are also student-athletes who have to leave school early because they do not have enough money to continue, or to pay their bills and leaving school for a career in professional sports is an easy way of making money. The argument is that if student-athletes get paid, they will remain in school and complete their education.

But, is money such a big problem for these student-athletes? Don't they receive scholarships? How much more money do they need? The truth is that "full" scholarships do not always entirely cover tuition and cost of living. However, these students can still do what a majority of students do, which is to get loans. Still, some of these student-athletes do not qualify for such loans, so there is still a gap between the money they get and the total cost of attendance. This gap, coupled with the fact that football and basketball players help generate so much revenue, has caused some intercollegiate teams to provide their athletes with extra compensation, which is in direct violation of National Collegiate Athletic Association (NCAA) bylaws.

Perhaps creating a method of payment above and beyond scholarships would help to decrease the amount of corruption, and "under the table" activities of some of these nationally recognized sports programs. But creating such a system may also lead to other problems. Developing such an economy in college football and basketball would result in a monetary race to buy the best athletes in the country. This would lead to a significant gap in talent between rich schools and poor schools. The disparity would result in a lack of competition, and may result in "Cinderella" teams [teams that rise from hardship] becoming a thing of the past. The more the disparity, the less the competition, and the less the competition, the less excitement. Less excitement will result in less revenue, and less revenue means less money for collegiate programs other than basketball and football. Ultimately, however, the main concern with paying athletes should not be one of establishing competitive balance and preserving "Cinderella" teams.

Education Ahead of Hired Entertainers

The main problem with paying student-athletes is that it is not the college's primary function. The primary function of academic institutions is to educate, and not to hire student-athletes for their contributions on the basketball court or football field. Moreover, colleges already provide student-athletes with an invaluable benefit. This benefit comes in the form of a college degree, which gives students opportunities in the job market that they would otherwise not have had. These basketball and football programs also provide some student-athletes the opportunity to get excellent educations for which they normally would not have been qualified, or have applied. These programs also give student-athletes the opportunity to become professional athletes. Moreover, most of these sports programs have been around long before present-day student-athletes began to participate in them. How much of the financial success can be attributed to the players, especially in college sports, where a team's success is largely dependent on the coach's and his or her staff's abilities?

Many of these programs were profitable long before some of these players arrived, and some of these players probably chose a particular program because of their past success. These players may have chosen a school due to the amount of scholarship money they were receiving, but scholarship money is usually not enough to overwhelm other considerations such as a school's academic standing, the coach's leadership and teaching skills, and a school's reputation. Paying student-athletes any more than a scholarship would put such considerations in jeopardy, resulting in students making decisions based on how much money they are offered, as opposed to making decisions based on where they will succeed in all aspects of college life. The college experience, a student-athlete's educational experience should be about more than just dollars and cents.

Facilitating Education for Athletes

Despite the strength of the reasons as to why student-athletes should not be paid, there are certain problems with the current NCAA system which can and should be cured. The gap between a full scholarship and the cost of attendance should be covered by the academic institution, especially when a student athlete does not qualify for a loan. Such a policy will go a long way in ensuring that student-athletes are not leaving school to become professional athletes because they cannot pay their bills. Academic institutions should be able to provide at least that much for their athletes. Ultimately, this is a form of payment, but it is not the type of payment that some individuals are advocating. The primary purpose of these institutions is to educate; it is the coach's job to teach, and not just in terms of the sport a student athlete plays. These schools should facilitate the educations of student-athletes through scholarship grants, but not through a system of salaries dependent on supply and demand, which ultimately detracts a student-athlete from picking a school, and detracts them from attending a school, for the right reasons.

3

College Athletes Should Not Be Paid due to Post-Eligibility School Benefits

Eugene McCormack

Eugene McCormack is a staff editor for the Chronicle of Higher Education.

Much is made of the limits that are placed on the time and re-sources of college athletes while they are participating in their chosen sport at the university level. However, there are many programs that help pay for the costs of college athletes to return to school after their playing careers have concluded. Colleges even have incentives to help former athletes get their degrees un-der recently enacted rules by the National Collegiate Athletic As-sociation that allow schools to count degrees by former athletes towards their graduation mandates.

When C. J. Masters dropped out of Kansas State University in March 1993, he was just six classes shy of a de-gree in criminology. The starting safety on the 20th-ranked football team wanted to devote all of his energy to the forth-coming National Football League draft.

For months Mr. Masters flew from city to city, trying out for teams in three professional leagues. When no one offered

Eugene McCormack, "Classroom Comeback," *The Chronicle of Higher Education*, vol. 52, July 7, 2006. Copyright © 2006 by *The Chronicle of Higher Education*. This article may not be published, reposted, or redistributed without express permission from The Chronicle.

him a contract, he moved to Kansas City, where, over the next few years, he held several low-paying jobs, including organizing schedules and appointments at a group home for troubled adolescents.

During the late 1990s, he tried his hand at sales, but never felt fulfilled. Then, in 2002, he learned about a job helping children with developmental disabilities, and was hired as a case manager.

He loved working with kids. But over the next few years, he was passed over for several higher-paying jobs because he didn't have a college degree. In late 2004, he called Kansas State's athletics officials to see what they could do to help him earn his diploma.

What Mr. Masters and hundreds of former college athletes have discovered in recent years is that many institutions— including Marshall University, the University of Kentucky, and the University of Nebraska at Lincoln—are making it easier for college athletes to complete the degrees that eluded them during their playing days.

Although thousands of athletes who left college early have returned during the past two decades, the numbers have recently spiked. Athletics officials attribute some of the growth to a new incentive from the National Collegiate Athletic Association that rewards teams when former athletes come back.

Under the NCAA's Academic Progress Rate formula, which measures how well teams are performing in the classroom, teams with low scores can lose scholarships. But when former players return to complete their degrees, teams earn bonus points that can help them avoid such penalties.

The incentive has spurred some colleges to reach out to former athletes as never before, offering free tuition, housing, and other assistance—often in exchange for part-time work in the athletics department.

Academic Officials' Mixed Views

Academic officials are happy to see former athletes return, as many show a newfound focus on their studies. But some critics say the change in attitude only proves that colleges put big-time athletes under too much physical and emotional strain to concentrate on their class work.

"Athletes returning to school is a positive step because the discipline that they learned in sports, they finally can apply to their course work," says Murray Sperber, professor emeritus of English and American studies at Indiana University at Bloomington and author of several books on college sports. "But the fact that athletes usually perform better academically when their eligibility is over shows the huge flaw in the current system."

Under NCAA rules, students may receive athletics aid for no more than five years in a six-year period, and many players in the NCAA's top division do not finish in that time. But students who come back for their degrees may qualify for NCAA grants or tuition assistance.

Many colleges that provide financial help to returning athletes are members of the National Consortium for Academics and Sports. Started in 1985, the program has helped thousands of former players finish their degrees at no cost to themselves, though they must participate in community-service projects for 10 hours a week. Colleges pay a small fee to join the consortium and cover the cost of the returning students' tuition.

As athletes have returned, some have helped their alma maters avoid NCAA penalties.

Athletics officials credit the consortium with helping them bring back the majority of former athletes who have completed their degrees in recent years. But some colleges say the

NCAA's new academic incentive has led them to redouble their efforts, or start new programs, to bring players back.

From 2003–4 to 2004–5—the first two years that the NCAA has kept track of returning athletes—there was a 23-percent increase in the number of students who came back, with a total of 849 former players in the top division re-enrolling in those two years to finish their degrees.

More than half—58 percent—of those students played baseball, football, or men's basketball in college. That is no surprise, several experts say, as graduation rates in those sports are usually among the lowest.

Football players have returned in droves. In fact, 38 percent of all NCAA Division I football programs have had at least one player come back to finish his degree in the two most recent academic years.

Several universities say they are motivated to bring former athletes back because the students made many sacrifices for their institutions.

As athletes have returned, some have helped their alma maters avoid NCAA penalties. This spring [2006] was the first time the association stripped scholarships from teams that underperformed academically. According to the NCAA, 265 teams were at risk of being penalized.

Fifty of those teams avoided punishment with a combination of retention adjustments and graduation bonus points they received from returning athletes' finishing their degrees. One-third to one-half of those 50 teams, the NCAA estimates, got around penalties solely through graduation bonuses.

Searching Databases

Several universities say they are motivated to bring former athletes back because the students made many sacrifices for their institutions. Officials at the University of Texas at Austin, where 30 to 40 players have returned in the past five years, and at the University of Maryland at College Park, which has brought back about 25 former players in the same period, say that helping athletes is simply the right thing to do.

"These individuals have spent four to five years at our university and have given us a lot," says Anton E. Goff, an assistant athletics director for academic support at Maryland. "We know the importance of getting an education, and if we can help them get one, we will."

The NCAA Incentive

But some institutions, including Marshall University, say they developed a plan to bring back former athletes primarily to boost their teams' academic-progress rates.

Last year Marshall officials started searching their database for athletes who had left campus within the past 10 years but needed less than one-year of credits to graduate. The university found that about a dozen former students, some of whom now play professional sports, were already eligible for diplomas—sometimes in different majors than they had signed up for. One former student who plays in the NFL got his degree simply by paying $100 in campus parking tickets.

To help students with 12 or fewer credit hours left to complete, the university has set up a program allowing students to work 20 hours a week in the athletics department to cover their tuition and living expenses. Two athletes have graduated under the plan, which began in August.

Marshall officials are not sure how much their returning students will help them avoid possible NCAA penalties once the returning graduates are factored into their scores.

Marshall's success in finding athletes close to earning their degrees has persuaded the university to start looking back 20 years to see if more players might need only a few classes to graduate.

Back After 20 Years

Other universities have already helped students come back after an absence of more than 20 years. Clifford Moller, a former basketball player at the University of Nebraska at Lincoln, left the Cornhuskers program after his junior year, in 1970, and returned to New York City, where for five years he drove a cab and installed telephone lines. Then, over the next 20 years, he worked in the real-estate business, eventually overseeing a 13-acre redevelopment project in Manhattan.

The project made him want to learn more about economic development, but he realized he needed a college degree to work in that field. He planned to go back to college in New York, but when he called Nebraska for his transcript, an academic adviser told him about a university program that helped former athletes. Mr. Moller learned that the university, a member of the National Consortium for Academics and Sports, would waive the cost of his tuition, fees, and books if he worked 12 hours a week as a study-hall counselor for athletes.

Mr. Moller says the offer was too good to pass up, and he returned to Lincoln in 1997, at age 47. Over the next three years, he sat through athletes' study halls four nights a week, telling students that they should focus on their studies to avoid ending up like him. "I would point to all the gray hairs on my head and say they don't want to be doing this when they're my age," he says.

Without basketball to distract him, Mr. Moller says, he dedicated himself to academics like never before, raising his grade-point average from 1.3 to 2.9 and finishing his undergraduate degree in communications in three years.

He went on to complete a master's degree in community and regional planning in 2003 and is now executive director of an economic-development association in Alexandria, La.

Paying for Scholarships

But many colleges do not have the money to help former athletes finish their academic work. Southern Utah University, for example, is more focused on securing a fifth year of aid for scholarship players than on trying to bring back athletes who did not graduate, says Myndee Larsen, an assistant athletics director.

"We're not even close to having the ability to look beyond that right now," she says.

As Mr. Masters, the former Kansas State football player, discovered when he called the university in the spring of 2005, even some big-time athletics programs do not offer financial incentives for returning athletes. But university officials helped him secure a $2,000 NCAA grant. Athletics officials also told him about the department's Second Wind program for comeback players.

Athletic departments that help pay for returning athletes do so with revenue from ticket sales, donations, and other sources.

The program provides former athletes assistance in scheduling classes and finding housing. If students don't want to move back to Kansas, the program allows them to take classes online or at other colleges and have the credits count toward their degree at Kansas State.

Mr. Masters was living in Phoenix and didn't want to move. Last summer he returned to Kansas to take one class, and over the past year he completed three courses online and two at Scottsdale Community College, near his home. He finished his criminology degree in May.

This fall or next spring, Mr. Masters plans to enroll in a Kansas State master's program in youth and development administration. He still wants to work with children, but he would like to find a position in a public parks-and-recreation department, setting up and running an after-school program or creating better designs for parks.

Giving the Revenue Back

Athletic departments that help pay for returning athletes do so with revenue from ticket sales, donations, and other sources. Athletics officials at Northeastern University say they receive about $100,000 a year from the university's student-financial-services budget to bring back about 10 former players. Other institutions have set up endowments to offset scholarships and other expenses.

The University Kentucky has established a fund in honor of Cawood Ledford, a former men's basketball announcer who died in 2001, to provide scholarship assistance to athletes who want to complete their degrees. To qualify for aid, players must work 20 hours a week in the athletics department and perform community-service work.

Since the fund was started, in 1992, it has helped more than 40 students, including the basketball star Allen Edwards, finish their educations. Mr. Edwards helped Kentucky win two national championships in the late 1990s, then left to play professionally for several years. He returned with financial assistance from the fund and finished his undergraduate work in sociology in 2002 with an eye toward becoming a college basketball coach. Now he is an assistant men's coach at Virginia Commonwealth University.

4

College Athletes Should Be Allowed To Have Their Own Endorsement Deals

Shelly Anderson

Shelly Anderson is a sports columnist for the Pittsburgh Post-Gazette.

Jeremy Bloom was a talented football player for the University of Colorado and also a talented skier who competed in the World Cup Championships and the Olympics. The National Collegiate Athletic Association (NCAA) ruled Bloom had violated its rules on college athletes having their own endorsement deals because Bloom accepted endorsement deals as a skier. Bloom could no longer play college football. It was hypocritical for the NCAA to take such a position since it allows other athletes to compete in college football while at the same time playing professional base-ball.

B lame it on the moguls.

Not the manicured bumps in the snow that Jeremy Bloom skis over so deftly on courses that would eat most people's knees for lunch.

The problem is with the big shots who make the rules.

Bloom is an accomplished two-sport athlete. While that's not rare, his combination of disciplines is unusual and, unfortunately for him, unworkable for now.

This 23-year-old Colorado native is the reigning World Cup champion in moguls freestyle skiing and is nearly a lock to make the United States Olympic team for the Turin Games in February [2006].

He finished ninth in the 2002 Olympics in Salt Lake City, beginning that year on the C team.

Two Sports, One NCAA

It's his other sport that was yanked away from Bloom.

He showed promise in two seasons with the University of Colorado football team. He was a Football Writers Association of America Freshman All-American in 2002, when he set a Buffaloes record with a 94-yard touchdown reception and scored on a 75-yard punt return.

Then, the NCAA rose its ugly head.

Once he realized his immense skiing potential, Bloom tried to sue the NCAA over its ban on endorsement money and eventually decided to defy the rule by taking on sponsors. It was either that or give up skiing.

Because Bloom accepted endorsements for skiing, the NCAA ruled him ineligible for college sports. Bloom and Colorado appealed, and he was careful to make sure his sponsors were not football-related and did not make any references to that sport, but the NCAA's final word came in August 2004.

Because Bloom was stuck between the NCAA's rules and those of the United States Olympic Committee [USOC], he missed the chance to play football as an upperclassman.

"That was the worst part," Bloom said. . . .

"I did all these things to prepare and I worked hard and the one thing I really wanted was to start at receiver. To look back and think that it wasn't my ability that kept me from doing that, it was an organization . . . I thought that was really unfair."

Bloom was a guest on the Buffaloes' sideline for homecoming Saturday when they beat Texas A&M, 41–20, to break into the national polls. Ideally, he would have redshirted this year to concentrate on skiing, then played his senior season in 2006.

There is no good reason he shouldn't have been able to do that.

When the Bloom situation came up, it would have been an ideal time for the NCAA to revisit its stance.

The USOC long ago had to give in and let athletes accept endorsement money because that's the only way it could afford to compete internationally. Now, even top pro athletes are eligible for the Games.

Amateurs? Be Real

The NCAA's rules on endorsements are rooted in its athletes being amateurs. But let's be real.

Overlooking the fact that full-scholarship athletes get a big return on their performance in the form of tuition, room, board and sometimes celebrity and a shot at a pro career, the NCAA reeks of hypocrisy because it allows some dual-sport athletes to have pro careers, as with many college football players who have played pro baseball.

There is no justifiable difference between a college football player being allowed to accept pay for competing in one sport and his being allowed to accept endorsement money for competing in another.

When the Bloom situation came up, it would have been an ideal time for the NCAA to revisit its stance. Instead, it stubbornly stood behind an outmoded rule.

"The NCAA can't keep turning a cold shoulder on athletes," Bloom said.

To its credit, the USOC is attempting to get the NCAA to listen.

Bloom said Jim Scherr, CEO of USOC, is helping to write proposals to the NCAA that would assist future college-Olympic dual-sport athletes.

To be fair, Bloom's life hasn't been ruined by the NCAA. He has become something of a pinup man, winning the 2003 made-for-TV "SuperStars" competition (he donated his prize money to charity) and getting a spread in GQ magazine. He might have a future as a model or actor.

That's beside the point, though. His college football career didn't have to be cut short.

The Dream Is Still Alive

Bloom still pines for football. He has his eye on the NFL [National Football League] pre-draft combine workouts about a week after he hopes to earn an Olympic medal in Italy.

He has started interviewing with agents and hopes to choose one by next week. A front-runner is Leigh Steinberg, who represents Steelers quarterback Ben Roethlisberger.

Bloom said he hopes to talk to Roethlisberger soon for advice and that, someday, he dreams of catching a pass from someone like Roethlisberger.

His chances of that would be better if he had completed a successful college career, but that's not Bloom's fault.

Editor's Note: Jeremy Bloom was never able to play football at the University of Colorado again. He went on to win the World Cup Championships in the moguls event in 2005 and placed sixth at the 2006 Turin Olympics. After the Olympics he decided to make football his top priority and was taken by the Philadelphia Eagles in the 2006 NFL draft. However, he had to sit out the 2006 season with an injury.

College Athletes Should Be Paid As Schools Neglect Their Academic Interests

Tom Palaima

Tom Palaima is Dickson Centennial Professor of Classics at the University of Texas at Austin. He is also a frequent contributor to the Austin-American Statesman.

Football players at the University of Texas (UT) have a low graduation rate. Colleges do not always look out for the best interests of their players academically, and players can fall through the cracks. It is also more likely that college basketball players will be going to school just to play basketball rather than get an education since the National Basketball Association passed a rule that a player must be nineteen years old or his high school graduating class must have been out of school for at least one year to be eligible to play professionally.

The University of Texas at Austin NCAA [National Collegiate Athletic Association] sports programs have been in the national spotlight. In early October [2006], the chairman of the U.S. House Ways and Means Committee sent the president of the NCAA a letter containing 25 detailed questions about funding practices and educational values in big-time college athletics.

UT was singled out for its low six-year graduation rate in football. It is 29 percent or 40 percent, depending on whether the federal government or the NCAA is doing the calculating.

Even figured generously, three out of five football players who play in Royal-Memorial Stadium do not receive a degree from any institution of higher education within six years. But statistics, even casualty figures from Iraq, mean little to most of us, unless they are personalized.

What Happened to Ramonce Taylor?

A recent sad case of this use-them-and-lose-them practice is Ramonce Taylor. Right before the Rose Bowl last year, in a *Daily Texan* story titled "Ramonce Taylor is Texas' Reggie Bush," head coach Mack Brown heaped praise on Taylor. "Ramonce has steadily become our Reggie Bush. He is a guy who every time he touches it, he has a chance to score." Imagine the effect on an impressionable football-focused sophomore to be compared by his coach to an eventual Heisman trophy winner.

Taylor scored a touchdown in the Rose Bowl. It turned out to be his last one as a Longhorn. In early March, before the start of spring practice, coaches announced that he had academic problems he needed to work on. Last year, we witnessed the miraculous transformation of junior basketball star P. J. Tucker. In a widely publicized story, Tucker, with the help of a battery of tutors and advisers, went from academic ineligibility and a self-admitted lifelong disregard for academics to a 3.3 fall-semester GPA [grade point average]. That one semester earned him UT's Academic Services Student-Athlete Award. During spring semester, he left UT for the NBA [National Basketball Association].

There was no such good-PR happy ending for Taylor. The next time he made the headlines, he had been arrested in May in connection with a large quantity of marijuana. No matter. Coach Brown declared that Texas was clean. Taylor had already been excused from the team for academic reasons and would not be reinstated.

Is anyone looking out for the academic well-being of young athlete-students?

I have taught at universities for 30 years, including another top sports school, the University of Wisconsin. Academic problems do not only become apparent weeks after an athlete-student has scored 15 touchdowns in his sophomore season. In the old days, it was possible to look at what classes athlete-students were taking and what grades they were making. No more. The Family Educational Rights and Privacy Act furnishes college sports programs with a protective shield.

You and I will never know what Taylor's transcript looked like. But the demands of BCS-level [Bowl Championship Series] competition and his coach's lavish praise of his athleticism did not help him stay on track toward a degree.

Some Help from the NBA

Is anyone looking out for the academic well-being of young athlete-students? The NBA and NCAA would like us to think they are. The NBA recently introduced a rule prohibiting talented young players, such as LeBron James, from going professional right out of high school. Now, they have to be mature 19-year-olds, and their graduating classes have to have been out of high school for a year.

The NBA rule is designed to protect the quality-of-play of NCAA teams and thereby their television-broadcast revenues.

However, sportswriters and sports Web sites have unmasked this fraud. The NBA rule is a bonanza for NCAA sports. The *Denver Post* on Saturday [November 11, 2006] identified the UT Longhorns basketball team as big winners: "Texas hit the jackpot with 6–9 swingman Kevin Durant, who has skills from the paint to the 3-point line. He is so good a Texas newspaper boasted 'the next time they redecorate the Erwin Center, University of Texas officials might want to display prominently a portrait of (NBA Commissioner) David Stern.'"

Two days earlier in the *American-Statesman*, Durant declared that his being barred from the NBA was "a blessing in disguise." He was enthusiastic about how much he could learn, about basketball, "in four more months" before turning pro. When pressed, he said, "Maybe I'll leave this year; maybe I'll leave next year."

The Rent-a-Player Program

It would be nice if the NCAA were to give coaches in its bent-on-winning programs instruction manuals on how to maintain the pretense that these rent-a-players are focusing on their intellectual and cultural improvement in the 1 1/2 to 3 1/2 semesters they spend on college campuses.

The NBA rule is designed to protect the quality-of-play of NCAA teams and thereby their television-broadcast revenues. It also saves NBA teams millions of dollars in salaries rising stars would receive while they are being developed. College athletes work for scholarship stipend money.

But it violates the economic rights of 18-year-old athletes. Why force them to spend parts of one or two years on college campuses masquerading as students?

My own vain hope is that some enterprising law professor here at UT, let's call him or her the anti-Joe—Jamail, will step forward and file a class-action suit against the NBA and the NCAA—and maybe even against UT athletics as accessories after the fact.

6

College Athletes Should Not Be Paid Because They Are Not Exploited

Jon Saraceno

Jon Saraceno is a sports columnist for USA Today.

Some college athletes complain that they are exploited because they produce large amounts of revenue for their universities but are not allowed to share in those monies beyond what is provided in their basic scholarship. The college sports system has its flaws, but the athletes are not exploited. Athletes get a chance to become known in their sport among professional teams and fans while getting the opportunity for an education that could be worth $100,000 or more. Advocates of paying players also need to realize that most colleges could not afford to do so, and the Title IX federal law would require that all athletes in all sports be paid, regardless of how much revenue they produce.

When Florida's Joe Cohen heard about the $32 million megadeal Alabama awarded its new football coach this week [January 2007], he was delighted. "I'm happy for Nick Saban," said the Gators senior defensive tackle. "That's a lot of money. *Somebody* has to get paid."

Coaches get richer. Schools and conferences rake in millions of sponsorship and television dollars for the Bowl Championship Series [BCS]. Networks reap the rewards of higher ratings. College ledgers benefit, too.

And the student-athletes?

"I think, in all honesty, one of the most exploited groups of people (in the USA) are college athletes," said Ohio State flanker Anthony Gonzalez, who might turn pro.

"We basically have a job that generates millions and millions and millions of dollars. At the end of the day, we don't really see it. That's the reality. There is nothing you can do about it."

Hitting the Jackpot

Florida and Ohio State equally will rack up a national championship game jackpot worth about $36 million, though they will share the windfall with schools from their respective conferences.

Football jerseys fly off the rack in Columbus, Ohio, and Gainesville, Fla., without players receiving a cent of the merchandising revenue. The NCAA [National Collegiate Athletic Association] is a tax-exempt organization that operates as a monopoly, its rulebook denser than the New Testament. Meanwhile, the NFL [National Football League] enjoys fruits of a minor league feeder system.

Recently, there was a big fuss when a spaghetti dinner was arranged to raise money so some parents of Buckeyes players could travel to Arizona. Red flags immediately were raised because it was believed the dinner might violate NCAA regulations and put players in jeopardy for Monday's championship game. (It didn't.)

The issue of pay-for-play has been around for decades. And, certainly, there's the old yarn about collegiate stars leaving certain academic institutions and having to take a pay cut when they reach the NFL.

Ideally, these guys should be paid. Then again, in a perfect world, we wouldn't have the BCS, either.

Exploitation?

The word "exploit" conjures up many negative images. A young athlete receiving an education worth more than $100,000 at many out-of-state universities, along with his BMOC [Big Man On Campus] status, isn't one of them.

"I don't know if I would say exploited," Buckeyes coach Jim Tressel said. "We have 36 sports of almost 1,000 athletes, most of whom who don't generate anything and they're getting a pretty good situation. Those that happen to be in the sports that do generate (money), I, for one, think you should be grateful you could help those other (athletes).

[Y]oung men are being plugged into an existing economic system that gives them, in essence, the chance to build their brand.

"I wouldn't say exploited. If that were the case, maybe 18-year-olds will go start a professional league and we'll see how they do."

That's the litmus test.

A Chance to Build a Brand

In other words, young men are being plugged into an existing economic system that gives them, in essence, the chance to build their brand. That's what Maurice Clarett was doing before he abused the system and submarined his future.

Asked whether college football players were taken advantage of, Ohio State quarterback Troy Smith threw it away. "I think that's a whole different world and we start a whole different kind of uproar. I'm going to pass on that question."

"I'd rather not preach on that topic," said teammate Antonio Pittman.

The work needed to stay eligible while performing what amounts to a full-time job is demanding and stressful. A monthly stipend seems reasonable, but Gonzalez acknowledged, "What would be fair would probably sink the whole idea of college football."

If college athletes are able to defer gratification, they can end up getting more than their fair share.

This week, as millions of dollars churned in various local economies because of the players' sweat equity, the Gators and Buckeyes players were tossed trinkets.

"We got some kind of radio, a throwback helmet, these sweats I'm wearing and a bag that says Tostitos Fiesta Bowl," said the Gators' Ray McDonald.

Most athletic departments operate budgets shaded in red. The largest, most successful schools, could afford to pay players, but what about the Timbuktu Techs?

Then there are the legal ramifications. With Title IX, every athlete has to be compensated in every sport.

That never will happen.

"I wouldn't say we were exploited, because we're getting a college education and we get all these perks," said Buckeyes safety Brandon Mitchell, who already has a degree in political science. "People say we should be paid, but I'm happy with a free education."

If college athletes are able to defer gratification, they can end up getting more than their fair share. The most valuable thing they receive is opportunity. There is no price tag anyone can place on that kind of investment.

7

Paid College Athletes Won't Be Tempted to Accept Illegal Payments or Gamble

Brian L. Porto

Brian L. Porto is an attorney and a professor. He is the author of May It Please the Court: Judicial Process and Politics in America *and* The Craft of Legal Reasoning. *His writings have also appeared in the* Journal of Sport and Social Issues.

College athletes are exploited by the universities they represent on the playing field. The athletes can see that everyone else is making money but they are not allowed to have any. This gives them incentives to accept illegal payments from boosters and agents or to enter into deals with gamblers to affect the outcome of games for betting purposes. The irony is that while universities may increase their exposure and recognition through big-time college sports, those institutions may end up losing their integrity and reputation in the process.

The social costs of college sports are high, . . . and increasingly, they also cry out for major change. One social cost of college sports is the exploitation of athletes by colleges and universities. A prominent example of athletic exploitation is colleges' history of using the physical talents of athletes for four years, then, when the athletes have exhausted their eligibility, casting them to the four winds without a degree or marketable skills other than athletic talent, which will take only a fortunate few to the NFL [National Football League] or to the NBA [National Basketball Association]. The principal victims of this type of exploitation have been African-American males, who are frequently the stars of college football and basketball teams but who are just as frequently casualties of big-time college sports, which their low graduation rates reflect.

Two related examples of athletic exploitation are freshman eligibility to compete in sports and annually renewable athletic scholarships, both of which began in the early 1970s. The NCAA [National Collegiate Athletic Association] made freshmen eligible for varsity competition in 1972, principally in order to save colleges the considerable expense of maintaining separate freshman teams, which had existed prior to 1972. Evidently, the needs of freshmen to make the often-difficult social, academic, and athletic transition from high school to college as smoothly as possible were not sufficiently compelling to override the needs of athletic directors to reduce the costs of their sports programs. In 1973, only a year after instituting freshman eligibility for varsity competition, the NCAA converted athletic scholarships, which had been four-year grants ever since their establishment in 1956, into one-year, annually renewable grants.

Under these circumstances it is not surprising that athletes try to exploit their own athletic ability for financial rewards.

Taken together, freshman eligibility and annually renewable athletic scholarships turn the NCAA's ideal of the "student-athlete" on its head. They force college students who play varsity sports to be athletes first and students second, if at all. Freshman eligibility in this television-driven era results in freshman football players at Division I-A colleges playing in regular-season football games before they have attended college classes. Annually renewable scholarships mean that some of those freshmen will lose their access to a college education before sophomore year begins because they have failed to satisfy their coaches' expectations. If requiring a college student to play a football game before his first class meets and depriving him of access to a college education because of his athletic deficiencies are not exploitation, then the NCAA has redefined that word, and my dictionary is obsolete. My dictionary says that *to exploit* is "to take advantage of" or "to use selfishly for one's own ends," and that is what freshman eligibility and annually renewable scholarships enable colleges to do to their athletes.

Student-Athletes?

Ironically, the NCAA invented the term "student-athlete" in support of its insistence that college football and basketball players are students and amateur athletes, not employees of their colleges who are entitled to workers' compensation when injured on the job. The denial of workers' compensation benefits, or a comparable alternative, to athletes who have suffered serious injuries while playing for their colleges may be the most compelling evidence that the NCAA and its members exploit college athletes. To add insult to injury, annually renewable scholarships permit colleges not only to deny seriously injured athletes workers' compensation benefits but also to rescind their athletic scholarships if they are unable to play or to play up to the coach's expectations.

Under these circumstances it is not surprising that athletes try to exploit their own athletic ability for financial rewards. The behavior of the adults who run college sports signals that the games exist for the purpose of making money, so the athletes conclude that they should share in the profits for which their sweat and talents are responsible. NCAA rules prohibit them from sharing legally, but some do so illegally. In a 1989 survey of professional football players, 31 percent of the respondents admitted to having accepted illegal payments during their college careers, and 48 percent of the respondents said that they knew of other athletes who took such payments during college. Former North Carolina State University basketball player Charles Shackleford, who left school in favor of the NBA after his junior season, admitted to having accepted approximately $65,000 in illegal payments during his three years in Raleigh.

It is not uncommon for college football and basketball players to try to exploit their athletic status for financial gain through gambling.

These examples show that college athletes are not always victims; they can be villains, too. Recently, their villainy, which has often been criminal, has become a major social cost of big-time college sports. This is sad and disturbing, but it is no more surprising than athletes' acceptance of under-the-table payments from athletic boosters. If the pressures for institutional fame and fortune through sports can cause colleges to admit athletes who are academically deficient, surely those same pressures can and do cause colleges to admit athletes who are not solid citizens. Evidently, colleges admit such athletes routinely because newspaper sports pages report criminal behavior by college athletes with frightening regularly. . . .

Incentives to Gamble

Gambling by athletes is a growing social cost of big-time college sports. It reflects their conclusion that adults make money from college sports, so they should do so, too. This thinking is especially troublesome when it causes athletes to use their privileged positions in order to make money from gambling. According to a recent University of Michigan study, it is not uncommon for college football and basketball players to try to exploit their athletic status for financial gain through gambling. In January of 1999, *U.S.A. Today* reported the results of the Michigan study, which revealed that more than 5 percent of college football and men's basketball players have either given inside information about their teams to gamblers (usually their classmates), bet on games in which they have played, or shaved points in return for money. One athlete, former Northwestern running back Dennis Lundy, went so far as to fumble the football intentionally near the goal line during a close game with Iowa in 1994 in order to save his bet.

Ironically, Lundy's bet nullified what *New York Times* columnist Robert Lipsyte referred to as "Northwestern University's bet," during the mid-1990s, that the millions of dollars it had spent to improve its football and men's basketball teams, which were perennial doormats in the Big Ten Conference, "would pay off in national happy news, increased enrollment, and alumni donations." The payoff was brief; applications to Northwestern increased after the Wildcats' trip to the Rose Bowl in 1995 but declined again amidst the revelations of the gambling scandals in both football and men's basketball. The scandals enraged many Northwestern alumni, who are justifiably proud of their alma mater's lofty academic reputation; some alumni vowed not to contribute any money to Northwestern until it adopted a "sane athletics policy.". . .

The Price of Athletic Success

The athletic tail has wagged the academic dog on American campuses for decades during which the public has become cynical about the educational value of college sports. A 1991 survey by Louis Harris and Associates revealed that 75 percent of the 1,255 adults polled agreed: "Intercollegiate athletics have got out of control," and "In too many universities with big-time athletics programs the academic mission has not been given proper priority over the athletics program." A 1997 CBS News poll of 1,037 adults found that 47 percent of the respondents agreed that college sports were "overemphasized," as did 62 percent of the college graduates surveyed. Cynicism peaks when a scandal is revealed, and the offending college must hear the brunt of that cynicism. The comments of Rev. John LoSchiavo—who was the president of the University of San Francisco (USF) in 1982, when USF disbanded its basketball team as a result of NCAA violations by players and boosters—illustrate this point. According to Father LoSchiavo, "The price the university has had to pay for those problems has been much greater than the heavy financial price. There is no way of measuring the damage that has been done to the university's most priceless asset, its integrity and its reputation."

8

College Athletes Should Not Be Paid Because a College Education Is Valuable

James L. Shulman and William G. Bowen

James L. Shulman and William G. Bowen were both officers at the Andrew W. Mellon Foundation when they wrote, The Game of Life: College Sports and Educational Values. *They later helped to co-author a book titled* Reclaiming the Game: College Sports and Educational Values. *Shulman has also collaborated on several other books. Bowen is former president of Princeton University where he was also a professor of economics.*

Each college and university can only admit a limited number of students every year. The opportunity for a college education for many potential students is reduced every time the educational institution gives special preference in admitting athletes or holding spots open for them. There are some small, academically-focused colleges where a significant percentage of the admitted students are athletes who have lesser qualifications than most of the other applicants. Sometimes athletes do not appreciate the educational opportunities they are given, particularly if they view the college experience merely as an opportunity to prepare to play in a professional sports league. Research shows that the values athletes learn as a result of being involved in college sports may help them to obtain greater financial success after college than many other groups of students.

Much of this study has focused on spillover effects—the unintended by-products of the building of ambitious athletic programs under what are clearly admirable banners. In this chapter we seek first to summarize the major changes that have taken place and then to reflect upon the dynamics that have produced—and continue to fuel—the intense competition to excel in intercollegiate athletics at all levels of play.

A major unifying theme of this study is that an ever larger divide has opened up between two worlds. One is an ever more intense athletics enterprise—with an emphasis on specialized athletic talent, more commercialization, and a set of norms and values that can be seen as constituting a culture of sports. The other is the core teaching-research function of selective colleges and universities, with its own increasing specialization, a charge to promote educational values such as learning for its own sake, and a strong sense of obligation to provide educational opportunity to those who will make the most of it—all in a time when the good of the society is increasingly dependent on the effective development and deployment of intellectual capital. This widening athletic-academic divide—its pervasiveness and subtlety—is the core of this book's message. . . .

Rationing Educational Opportunity

Today, as in the 1920s, many of those who play college sports enjoy the experience and benefit from it. But supporting the extensive intercollegiate programs that exist today also entails substantial costs, and the most important may not be the readily apparent dollar outlays required to field teams, build facilities, and (in the case of the Division IA schools) provide athletic scholarships. One of the most valuable resources that the leading colleges and universities must ration is the limited number of places in each entering class. For the most academically selective schools, admissions is a zero-sum game: the more athletes who are recruited, the less room there is for other students.

The more difficult, and more relevant, question is whether admitting other students in their place might not have done even more to fulfill the educational mission of the school.

Recruiting athletes for up to 40 intercollegiate teams at colleges and universities that are vastly oversubscribed by talented applicants has major opportunity costs—especially at the smaller Ivy League universities and the coed liberal arts colleges. In this crucial respect, the consequences of athletic recruitment are far more serious for these schools than for large universities with big-time programs. In the words of a former president of a distinguished public university, "Yes, it was embarrassing when there was a scandal of one kind or another, but the number of athletes was so small relative to the size of the student body that whatever they did or didn't do in the classroom or on the campus didn't really affect the place as a whole." *Athletics is a much more serious business, in terms of its direct impact on admissions and the composition and ethos of the student body, at an Ivy League school or a coed liberal arts college than it is at a Division IA university.* This basic point is often overlooked. Highly publicized incidents at big-time schools get all the press—and they are very important for what they say to both campus communities and a broad public about the values of the institution—but the issues of direct educational consequence flowing from the recruitment of large numbers of athletes are much more serious at the schools where athletes constitute anywhere from 15 to 35 percent of the student body.

Unlike some situations in big-time sports, in which coaches and players are literally at each other's throats, highly visible athletes are arrested for beating up their girlfriends, or self-important boosters contribute to the exploitation of athletes without any thought for their well-being, there are no villains associated with this part of the story. In writing about the implications of athletic recruitment for the rationing of educational opportunity, we most emphatically do not mean to suggest that the athletes who are admitted are bad people, that they will not benefit from attending these schools, or that attending one of these institutions will fail to help them achieve their personal goals. The more difficult, and more relevant, question is whether admitting other students in their place might not have done even more to fulfill the educational mission of the school.

The greatly increased competition for places in the leading schools makes this question far more important today than it used to be. In 1929, when the Carnegie report warned about how athletics might represent a threat to educational opportunity, the Commission members could not have known how scarce and valued those opportunities would become over the course of the century. One factor in the increasingly competitive college admissions process is that, over the past fifty years, new players have been allowed into the game—as women, minority students, and individuals from all socioeconomic classes have been encouraged to seek places where previously they may not have been welcome. Moreover, as our society has moved increasingly toward a knowledge-driven economy, the pressure to obtain the best possible education and to obtain credentials that will open the right doors has become ever more intense. Many students could further their individual goals by attending great universities like the University of North Carolina at Chapel Hill and Columbia, or colleges like Wellesley and Williams, but only so many can attend each year. These schools provide a flexible pool of opportunity that can be utilized in many ways. In addition to the educational advantages that they offer are reputational advantages and the connections that one makes by attending these schools. Having a degree from a leading college or university is helpful in getting a job on Wall Street, getting into graduate school, or making connections in the art world. Deciding who should have such opportunities is extremely challenging, and the outcomes of the admissions process reveal a great deal about how a college or university truly sees—and pursues—its mission.

Taking Full Advantage of Academic Opportunities

Faculty often remark that the most discouraging aspect of teaching is encountering a student who just does not seem to care, who has to be cajoled into thinking about the reading, who is obviously bored in class, or who resists rewriting a paper that is passable but not very good. Such students are failing to take full advantage of the educational opportunities that these colleges and universities are there to provide.

It is not good enough ... just to get by. Respect for core academic values and the educational mission of these schools requires more than that.

Uninspired students come in all sizes and shapes, and no one would suggest that athletes are uniformly different from other students in this regard. But the evidence presented in this book does demonstrate a consistent tendency for athletes to do less well academically than their classmates—and, even more troubling, a consistent tendency for athletes to underperform academically not just relative to other students, but relative to how they themselves might have been expected to perform. *These tendencies have become more pronounced over time and all-pervasive: academic underperformance is now found among women athletes as well as men, among those who play the Lower Profile sports as well as those on football and basketball teams, and among athletes playing at the Division III level of competition as well as those playing in bowl games and competing for national championships.*

If we take seriously the notion that students should take full advantage of what are very scarce educational opportunities, evidence of high graduation rates should not end the conversation. It is not good enough, we believe, just to get by. Respect for core academic values and the educational mission of these schools requires more than that. Otherwise, colleges and universities are failing to put their most valuable resources—their faculty and their academic offerings—to their highest and best use. In the telling words of the Carnegie report of 1929, they are displaying "a negligent attitude toward the educational opportunity for which the college exists." They are not focused on fulfilling their educational missions. . . .

The Athlete Culture: Life After College

Including in the class a large number of highly recruited athletes has a number of other, less direct, effects on the rationing of opportunity since, as a colleague once put it, "people come in packages." In the case of men, in particular, we have seen that there is a strong correlation between being an athlete, having a strong interest in achieving financial success, seeing college as a means to this end, and pursuing careers in fields such as finance. The strong tendency for athletes to concentrate in the social sciences and to opt for business and communications majors (where they are offered) is clearly related to these goals, as is their subsequent tendency to enroll in MBA programs. More generally, the "athlete culture" has a set of norms, values, and goals that are coherent, largely independent of socioeconomic status, and different from those of other groups of students attending the same institutions. This culture has natural affinities with what University of Chicago economist Frank Knight has called the "business game." Games with clear goals and rules, where competitive instincts, team play, and discipline are rewarded, provide a link between the culture of sports and marketplace pursuits.

There is certainly nothing wrong with this confluence of the values of sports and those of the business world. Colleges and universities are surely right to take pride in the accomplishments of their graduates who succeed in the "business game.". . .

In an ideal world, we would suppose, schools would like to see a diversity of majors, values, and career choices among all subgroups of students. In our view, society is best served when the financial services sector "inherits" some students who have a deep commitment to understanding history and culture (rather than mainly those with a more narrow focus on earning a great deal of money as an end in and of itself). In the same way, academia benefits when some of those who pursue Ph.D.s also have learned some of the lessons about life that one gains on the playing fields (rather than just those with a more narrow focus on an arcane, if not obscure, realm of academic research). In short, the heavy concentration of male athletes, in particular, in certain fields of study raises real questions of institutional priorities and balance.

Allocating Financial Resources

If intercollegiate sports was self-financing and raised no resource allocation questions for colleges and universities, the issues discussed thus far would still be consequential. Unmeasured "costs," including especially the opportunity costs associated with admitting Smith but not Jones, matter enormously at academically selective institutions. But it is also true that intercollegiate athletics programs involve the expenditure of a great deal of money. We were surprised to learn how high the net costs are (after taking account of revenue offsets) at the vast majority of the schools in our study. An obvious question is whether so much money really needs to be spent to achieve the benefits of well-conceived athletic programs. This is an issue for colleges and universities of all kinds, not just for those that are academically selective.

Here we note only that students who might be interested in other extracurricular pursuits—putting out the school paper or acting on stage, for example—have no comparable, equally expensive, infrastructure supporting them. Each assistant football coach takes the place of the non-existent journalism coach who would indubitably make the campus paper even better than it is absent such coaching. Disproportionate funding follows disproportionate athletic recruiting and succeeds in enabling a level of professionalism—but only in one particular area. It is useful to remember that per student expenditures on *all* student services combined (including core functions such as the admissions office) are in the range of $2,000 to $3,000 at these institutions, as compared with athletic outlays of $8,000 per individual athlete in the Ivies, to take that one point of comparison.

As he altered the university's funding structure to provide more resources for the athletic program at Vanderbilt, Chancellor Joe Wyatt acknowledged the reality of competing claims on scarce funds. As long as unrestricted University funds are being used to subsidize athletics, he noted, "the long-term effect may be to seriously impair Vanderbilt's ability to invest in some critical educational and research programs. And there is little doubt that such an outcome could jeopardize Vanderbilt's standing among the best universities in the nation." Wyatt also drew attention to the findings of a survey of parents of current students that found that they placed the highest priority on the quality of teaching, the quality of the faculty, the emphasis on undergraduate education, and preparation for future employment. Parents were pleased with Vanderbilt's performance on these scales, but they were split on the question of whether Vanderbilt was doing a good enough job controlling costs. Although they were willing to pay more to improve educational quality, Wyatt observed, "It seems safe to conclude that real or perceived increases in cost that do not contribute directly to the priorities related to educational quality would not be well received by Vanderbilt parents.". . .

Institutionalization of Athletics in the Academy

Looking back at the history of college sports over the course of the 20th century, one of the most important changes can be seen clearly only with the help of a long-distance lens: intercollegiate sports have become institutionalized in institutions of higher education. Whereas athletics programs were once a wild stepchild held at arm's length from the schools, run mainly by the players themselves and their devotees, they have by now been thoroughly enfolded into the fabric of these institutions. In an effort to control excess and police the games, schools took charge. In doing so, it was assumed, the strength of the institution's discipline and sense of purpose would moderate the passions inspired by athletics. There was, however, always the risk that, having gained a solid foothold inside the walls, the troubling aspects of the athletics enterprise would affect the academy at the very time that the academy was working to control them. Sports once seen as merely an outlet for passions and energy or as a community-building ritual are now justified as a training ground for leaders, a school for character, or "the sweatiest of the liberal arts." While there are positive sides to taking sports so seriously, doing so also legitimizes a possible confusion between the dictates of the playing field and the lessons of the classroom.

In embracing intercollegiate athletes, colleges and universities gambled on their ability to "control the beast.". . .

For years, people have understood that one can view life as a game. "Play the cards that Fate deals you," we are often told. But the country's leading colleges and universities have a special role to play in shaping the game of life, in setting the values (as opposed to the rules) of the game. The role of these institutions is not simply to be a facilitator of what each individual who "wins" the preliminary heats of the competition (the admissions game) sees the game to be. Colleges and universities are tax-favored, not-for-profit institutions because society agrees that they have a broader role to play in a far more consequential societal game. These institutions are charged to resist the narrow impulses of the marketplace, as well as ideological and political strictures of every kind: they are meant to live, as E. M. Forster once described the poet Cavafy, "at a slight angle to the universe." Pursuing their academic mission will produce better filmmakers, journalists, medical researchers, and yes, better bankers and lawyers too. But this will be accomplished by accepting those whom the schools believe will make best use of their educational resources and by insisting on the validity of their own missions.

In embracing intercollegiate athletics, colleges and universities gambled on their ability to "control the beast"—to harness the energies and many good qualities of sports to their own purposes, rather than to be subverted by them. The open question is whether this gamble was a good one: whether colleges and universities can rise to the challenge of re-balancing objectives and strengthening what we regard as the purer values of athletic competition. Leaders of these venerable academic institutions have difficult choices to make.

9

College Athletes Should Receive Guaranteed Four-Year Scholarships

Kevin Blackistone

Kevin Blackistone is a sports columnist for the Dallas Morning News.

The current system for awarding athletic scholarships allows a coach to cancel a player's scholarship after one year if the coach does not like the way the player is performing athletically, regardless of how the player is doing academically. It would be better if scholarships were awarded on a four-year basis, so that athletes would be guaranteed a chance to spend four years working towards a degree regardless of how well they perform athletically. Rather than be treated as employees who can be fired at the behest of a coach, college athletes should be treated as students who can continue to matriculate as long as they are meeting the academic standards of the university they are attending.

One Baylor basketball player is dead. Another faces charges for his murder. How culpable for this tragedy, if at all, is the private, faith-based university in Waco that they attended? We don't know yet.

But there is a good chance that Patrick Dennehy would be alive and Carlton Dotson would be a free man if not for a change the NCAA [National Collegiate Athletic Association] implemented 30 years ago in its rules about awarding athletic

Kevin Blackistone, "One-and-Out No Way to Play Scholarship Game," *Dallas Morning News*, January 14, 2003. © 2003 The *Dallas Morning News*. Reprinted with permission of the *Dallas Morning News*.

scholarships. In 1973, the governing body of college sports did away with four-year scholarships in favor of one-year renewable grants.

For all intents and purposes, student-athletes at that moment became employees of the athletic department, unpaid employees at that. To be sure, one side effect of the rule change was that coaches who had scholarship athletes who were failing to live up to their dreams started cutting them loose, firing them. At the end of a disappointing season on the field or in the gym, they'd get called into a coach's office and told they were no longer wanted. Their scholarship was not getting renewed.

That was how Dennehy and Dotson wound up crossing paths in ousted Baylor basketball coach Dave Bliss' program. Bliss lured Dennehy from New Mexico to take the roster spot of Dotson, whose services Bliss no longer desired.

"Running Players Off"

In the college athletic industry, they call that well-known practice "running players off." How much it happens is anyone's guess. But it should never happen. A coach ought to decide a student-athlete's playing time. His continued matriculation should be left to the provost's office.

Michael Oriard, the Oregon State professor and former Notre Dame and NFL [National Football League] standout who authored *King Football*, says the one-year scholarship "is sort of the stealth bomb of college athletics."

It needs to be detonated.

Its biggest danger isn't the horrific occurrence at Baylor. Something so bizarre hadn't happened before, thank goodness, and isn't likely to happen again.

But if college athletics' keepers are really concerned about the student-athlete's ability to get a college education, they can underscore that with better educational insurance. A four-year scholarship linked to the academic office is better educational insurance than a one-year deal linked to a coach's whim.

The one-year deal is why voluntary out-of-season practices become mandatory, as if the college player is some NFL pro.

If a kid doesn't live up to athletic expectations, that's too bad. The coach should have to live with his poor assessment of athletic talent or inability to develop it. But the kid should be able to pursue his degree rather than having it treated like remuneration for his field goal percentage.

Blurring the Distinction

As the Drake Group, a faculty coalition led by one-time Tennessee whistler-blower Linda Bensel-Meyers, suggests: "The NCAA must first acknowledge how its scholarship policies have blurred the distinction between college athletes and professionals if its proposals for reform are to be taken seriously."

The NCAA could end the hypocrisy by allowing athletes to share in the profits, the Drake Group says. But rather than move to full-scale professionalism, the coalition sees "a far more practical alternative": the elimination of the renewable athletic scholarship.

The Drake Group wants need-based financial awards to replace athletic grants-in-aid, or have outstanding student-athletes treated like, say, outstanding student-thespians. After all, most college scholarships are need-based rather than grants. Once again: Why should student-athletes be treated not only differently, but more favorably?

Athletic scholarships were need-based when they were introduced in the first half of the 20th century. It wasn't until 1956 that the NCAA instituted the so-called "free ride," a scholarship paying only for room, board, tuition and fees. Scholarships effectively became binding contracts with the athletic department in the late '60s, when the NCAA said scholarships could be terminated for students who quit playing sports.

It's past time now to push the pendulum back the other way toward the classroom and away from the weight room.

Four-Year, Need-Based Scholarships

A four-year, need-based award for student-athletes is not merely the height of an idealistic thought. The smallest colleges and least commercial, those in Division III, use it. So do the Patriot League and the Ivy League, both of which play I-AA football but top-level basketball.

"The need-based model could work if everyone in a conference chose to stick to that principle," said Don Vaughan, Colgate's hockey coach-turned-interim athletic director. "The problem comes in that most of the conferences across the country have moved beyond that."

The need-based concept, however, is disappearing. Patriot League schools such as Colgate are slowly but surely changing the way they attract and reward student-athletes, getting more like everyone else. Colgate is in the first year of phasing in athletic scholarships instead of need-based aid for basketball players.

"It wasn't about money," said Vaughan. "We're not spending any more money. We're awarding it differently."

It's allowed the school to compete for students who otherwise fell between the cracks of being able to afford a Colgate education and qualify for financial aid. Its recruiting pool is deeper.

But Vaughan said the benefit and principle of need-based aid for college athletes hasn't been lost on Colgate administrators, which is one reason Patriot League football still doesn't allow athletic scholarships.

"Philosophically, there's merit to it," Vaughan said of need-based aid. "They're getting their aid because they need it, not because of athletics. As long as you fill out the paper, and you qualify, that aid is there for you.

"That's the one quality that stands out. At the end of the day, it isn't tied to athletic performance."

That's because the recipient is considered a student.

10

Athletic Scholarships Should Be Eliminated

John R. Gerdy

John R. Gerdy is also the author of The Successful Athletic Program: The New Standard, Sports in School: The Future of an Institution, *and* Sports: The All-American Addiction.

The current system of college athletics is broken because it is based on a professional sports model rather than an educational model. Rather than simply trying to reform the system, it must be completely restructured. One of the steps that needs to be taken is to eliminate athletic scholarships in favor of the institutional need-based aid that is available to all students. While this would result in some athletes receiving less money, it would actually empower them in their ability to get a college education because they would no longer find themselves beholden to coaches and athletic departments. Currently, a student's athletic scholarship can be cut after one year if a coach feels he or she is not performing well as an athlete. This puts the emphasis on winning games rather than earning degrees.

Higher education leaders have been trying to reform athletics for decades. Despite these efforts, Division I athletics continues to undermine the academic integrity and educational missions of our colleges and universities in very significant ways. At issue is not the value of elite athletics in our culture but whether our educational institutions should be saddled with the responsibility of developing elite athletes and sponsoring professional teams. Like trying to fit a round peg into a square hole, the professional sports model simply does not fit within the educational community. Rather than continuing to pound that peg, it is time to admit that sponsorship of elite, professional athletics should be left to the professional leagues. In short, it is time for colleges and universities to eliminate their departments of professional athletics.

The following bears mentioning again. While one of American higher education's strengths is its tremendous diversity of services, programs, opportunities, and missions, in the case of athletics, higher education may not be able to have it all. Division I athletics, *as currently structured and conducted* is not meeting the purposes for which it became a part of higher education. That being the case, we have a responsibility to dramatically restructure Division I athletics to do so or, if that proves impossible, eliminate it. The history of American higher education offers many examples of programs or departments that were downsized or eliminated when it became apparent that they had become obsolete, had failed to meet their purpose, or had become a drain on institutional resources.

That said, the root cause of college athletics' ills is not commercialism nor academic fraud but rather the mode—the professional sports model—that higher education has chosen to meet its business, education, and commercial goals. Professional athletics is simply not an appropriate business for higher education.

A New Road

In short, it is time to take a new road; a road that would require not simply strengthening eligibility standards but deconstructing the entire enterprise. Rather than trying to be all things to all people, higher education's responsibility in the cultural area of athletics should be twofold: first, to involve the maximum number of students in sports activities that can be enjoyed for a lifetime for purposes of promoting public health and, second, to provide entertaining but educationally based intercollegiate athletics.

Specifically, the professional model of intercollegiate athletics must be dismantled and rebuilt, not as a mirror of professional sports but in the image of an educational institution. To do so, the fundamental principle on which the professional sports model is built—pay for play—must be changed. Specifically, the athletic scholarship must be eliminated in favor of institutional, need-based aid.

[F]or many coaches, the scholarship has little to do with educational opportunity or financial need and everything to do with control.

Realizing change of this magnitude will be neither quick nor easy. It is, however, necessary. The higher education community must come together in a show of courage and confidence to halt the steady and destructive march of the win-at-any-cost professional model of intercollegiate athletics. It will require the courage and will of higher education leaders to act upon the fact that college athletics is higher education's property; not ESPN's or CBS's, not Nike's or Adidas's, not corporate America's, not the sports talk-show hosts', and not the crazed fan's in the stands. Because athletics is higher education's property, it is the higher education community alone that must establish the rules of the game, the values of the enterprise, and the principles upon which it will be presented to the public. The fact is, higher education leaders can make athletics look like and represent whatever they want. If these leaders are serious about reforming athletics, they must address the professional aspects of the enterprise. . . .

Freedom to Pursue an Education

At first glance, it would appear that eliminating athletic scholarships in favor of a need-based formula would not be in the best interest of student-athletes. However, if this proposal is judged upon what is in their best interest for the next fifty years of their lives, rather than the four or five years they are on campus, it becomes clear that eliminating the athletic grant will contribute significantly to athletes' chances of obtaining a well-balanced academic, personal, and athletic experience while in college.

An athletic scholarship represents a contractual agreement between the athlete and the coach, which allows coaches to view athletes as employees, bought and paid for by the athletics department. Thus, for many coaches, the scholarship has little to do with educational opportunity or financial need and everything to do with control. Athletic scholarships are a powerful means of keeping athletes focused upon athletic performance. If the athlete does not do what the coach wants, he can be "fired" because the athletic scholarship is a one-year agreement, renewable at the discretion of the coach.

A need-based financial aid agreement, however, is a contractual agreement between the student and the institution. It guarantees that the student will continue to receive his or her financial aid regardless of what transpires on the athletic fields. There is no more effective way to empower the athlete because it fundamentally changes the relationship between the athlete, the coach, and the institution. Under such a contract, the student is less beholden to the athletics department's competitive and business motives and thus freer to explore the wide diversity of experiences college offers.

Underpaid Employees

Critics will argue that athletes are already underpaid in relation to the amount of money they generate for the institution. In the current professional model, college athletes *are* underpaid. The NCAA differentiates its "employment" arrangement from the professional model by claiming that the "student-athlete's" compensation is in the form of an "educational opportunity." Regrettably, in far too many cases, this "educational opportunity" is a sham. Despite all the attempts at academic reform, the current, professional model of college athletics has evolved to a point where the barriers to earning that well-balanced educational experience have become too great. It is no wonder athletes feel they are underpaid. They are clearly not getting the deal that was sold to them when the coach sat in their living rooms and promised a quality, well-balanced, academic, social, and athletic experience. In the need-based financial aid model, a legitimate educational experience is, once again, a viable part of the compensation package. And the value of a well-rounded, academically rigorous, and hard-earned educational experience is priceless. . . .

[F]or too long the American system of athletics has catered to the narrow needs of a few elite athletes while shortchanging the vast majority of participants.

Further, the financial hardship on athletes resulting from the shift to a need-based aid system will be less than one might think. While many football and basketball athletes will be required to pay a portion of their educational expenses, those who qualify for "full need" will receive it. Almost all other sports operate on what is known as an equivalency system, where most receive only partial athletic scholarships. . . .

Elite Athletics Will Be O.K.

The inability to receive a full-ride athletic scholarship, . . . will drive all but those who are serious about being genuine students from college programs. And there is absolutely nothing wrong with that. Athletes who will go to school only if they receive a full ride and play immediately can pursue their athletic career through the club system or with a professional team. If at some point these changes shock the system into becoming more balanced and educationally focused, reinstituting freshman eligibility could be considered. But a shock is what the current system needs, and the combination of these two changes will provide it.

Many will be unable to get beyond the impact these changes will have on the elite athlete, with the question being where they will go to hone their athletic skills. In our sports-obsessed culture, there is little doubt their needs will be met. The fact is, for too long the American system of athletics has catered to the narrow needs of a few elite athletes while short-changing the vast majority of participants. While catering to the elite athlete might be appropriate for a club or professional team or league, it is inappropriate for an educational institution. The elite athlete will continue to flourish, as an alternative system or structure with highly competitive outlets to develop their athletic potential will surface.

In many sports, this shift is occurring already. The most obvious example is baseball, with its well-established minor league system. Interestingly, in the shadow of the minor league system, college baseball thrives. In soccer, tennis, swimming, and basketball, club sports are emerging to cater to the athletic needs of the elite. In basketball, the National Basketball Association (NBA) has established a developmental league with a minimum age limit of eighteen. Thus, a high school athlete, rather than attending college to refine his skills for the NBA, could move directly to the developmental league and proceed on to the NBA at age nineteen.

In short, the purpose of an educational institution should be more focused on providing legitimate educational opportunities for students who are interested in using athletics to supplement the educational process rather than elite athletes who view their stay on campus simply as a means of getting to the pros.

Besides, how much can athletes who are in school primarily to play sports really learn if they view college as nothing more than a way station on their steady march to the pros? Should we be wasting tax dollars and school resources on those who have little desire to learn? And why do we believe that college is for everyone or that if you want a college degree you must earn it by age twenty-two?

In the final analysis, a need-based aid system will help ensure a genuine, well-balanced educational experience for the athlete that offers far more long-term value than an athletic scholarship system that serves as a barrier to achieving a genuine educational experience. The fact is, receiving need-based aid resulting in a legitimate educational experience that leads to a meaningful degree is a far better deal than getting an athletic scholarship to cover the cost of an educational experience that is a sham.

Equal Access to What?

Some argue that eliminating athletic scholarships . . . will deny opportunity and limit access for many students, most notably, black athletes. The question is access to what? To the fields of competition or to a quality, well-balanced opportunity to earn a meaningful degree? With black basketball and football players generally graduating in the mid 30 to mid 40 percent range, respectively, earning an athletic scholarship under the current system is little more than an opportunity to play ball.

Given these results, the larger question is whether the athletic scholarship, and the tremendous influence coaches have over the athlete who receives one, serves to limit the ability of the athlete to have a well-balanced collegiate experience and earn a meaningful degree. After all, coaches are paid to win. As a result, their short-term interests (win next week's game) are often at odds with the athletes' long-term educational interests (earn a degree). This is simply the reality of the current system. How many more athletes would graduate if it were not for the excessive time, energy, physical, and emotional demands placed upon them from the athletics department; demands that, if not met, will result in the elimination of the scholarship? Rather than the athletic scholarship being the determining factor in earning a degree, it is more likely that athletes graduate in spite of the demands of being beholden to what amounts to a professional sports franchise. These young people are so motivated, smart, and determined, they will find a way to graduate with a need-based aid package as opposed to a full athletic scholarship.

[O]ur policies and daily actions must show very clearly that education is the primary purpose of our athletics departments. . . .

Further, the athletic scholarship has made our educational institutions complicit in perpetuating a dangerous and counterproductive cultural myth. Specifically, far too many parents and youngsters believe sports, rather than education, is the ticket to future success. The professional model of college sports reinforces the myth that the road to economic and personal prosperity is best attained by chasing athletic fame, glory, and financial reward rather than by obtaining a quality education. This impact is particularly prevalent in the black community. One only has to consider the previously mentioned NCAA graduation rates to realize that, in most cases, this is a cruel hoax. While moving to a club system for elite athletics may not significantly change this myth, one thing is certain: our educational institutions should have absolutely no part in perpetuating it.

While the argument that the elimination of the athletic scholarship will inhibit some black athletes' ability to access higher education is powerful, a more likely result of this change will be that these black athletes will simply be replaced by other black athletes. While they may be a bit less talented and obsessed with athletics, they will likely be better students or at least more interested in academic achievement than in using the university as a springboard to the pros. In the end, more athletes, black, white, and Hispanic, will obtain a well-balanced college experience resulting in graduation. . . .

In the Interest of Athletes

In the final analysis, if we have the long-term academic and personal interests of young people in mind, the athletic scholarship should be eliminated in favor of a system that assures them a legitimate opportunity to actualize the personal, academic, athletic, and economic opportunities afforded by a well-balanced college education. Specifically, our policies and daily actions must show very clearly that education is the primary purpose of our athletics departments and that the true measure of success hinges upon obtaining a degree.

11

College Athletes Should Receive a Scholarship Raise to Cover Necessities

National College Players Association

The National College Players Association (NCPA) was formed by former UCLA football player Ramogi Huma in 2001. The purpose of the NCPA is to be an advocacy group that advocates for the rights of college athletes who are governed by the the rules of the National Collegiate Athletic Association (NCAA).

There is a difference between what is covered in a "full-ride" athletic scholarship and the actual costs of attending college. The National Collegiate Athletic Association (NCAA) acknowledges that the amount provided in an athletic scholarship is not enough to provide for many things a typical college student needs. The scholarship amount should be increased to meet the "cost of attendance" amount that universities list for students who are not on scholarship. This could be paid for out of the profits colleges earn from post-season tournaments.

Editor's Note: Former college football player Ramogi Huma formed the National College Players Association (NCPA) in 2001 as an advocacy group designed to promote and protect the rights of college athletes who are subject to the rules of the National Collegiate Athletic Association (NCAA). The following are the 10 goals of the NCPA.

National College Players Association (NCPA), "CAC Mission & Goals," cacnow.org, 2007. Reproduced by permission.

1. Raise the Scholarship Amount to Cover Necessities

The NCAA admits that a "full scholarship" does not cover the basic necessities for a student-athlete. The NCAA refuses to change its rules to allow schools to provide scholarships that equal costs. Each school lists the "cost of attendance" as the amount that all students need to survive financially and academically. A relatively small percentage of post-season revenues can be used to assist universities in providing scholarships that cover costs.

2. Secure Health Coverage for All Sports-Related Workouts

The NCAA does not require schools to pay for sports-related injuries—it's optional. Student-athletes injured during sports-related workouts should not have to pay for medical expenses out of their own pockets. Universities should be mandated to ensure that their student-athletes receive adequate medical care for all sports-related workouts, and should be free to provide additional health coverage as they see fit.

3. Increase Graduation Rates

The ultimate goal for a student-athlete is not a scholarship, it's a degree. The graduation rate for Division I football players hovers around 50% while men's basketball players graduate at a rate of about 40%. The NCAA can help improve these rates by awarding a significant portion of the NCAA basketball tournament to schools with the best graduation rates. In addition, the NCAA should work to reduce games that take place during the week. Although weekday games are in the interest of the TV networks, they hurt student-athletes academically.

4. Allow Universities to Grant 4-Year Scholarships Instead of 1-Year Revocable Scholarships

University recruiters mislead high school recruits by offering them 4-year scholarships even though the NCAA does not allow 4-year scholarships. The NCAA only allows 1-year scholarships that a university can revoke or renew for any reason (including injuries or personality conflicts). A university should be able to give 4-year scholarships and guarantee it in writing if it so chooses. This would help further protect student-athletes and end the deception in the recruiting process.

5. Prohibit Universities from Using a Permanent Injury Suffered During Athletics as a Reason to Reduce or Eliminate a Scholarship

Such actions reduce the chance for such student-athletes to graduate. Student-athletes put their bodies and lives on the line in their pursuit of higher education and the success of their university's athletic program. It is immoral to allow schools to eliminate a student-athlete's scholarship just because he/she can no longer perform.

6. Establish and Enforce Uniform Safety Guidelines in All Sports to Help Prevent Avoidable Deaths

Several deaths in college football off-seasons highlight the need for year round safety requirements that provide an adequate level of protections for student-athletes from all sports. Student-athletes and athletic staff should be given the means to anonymously report breaches in such guidelines.

7. Eliminate Restrictions on Legitimate Employment

Student-athletes should have the same rights to secure employment as other students and US citizens. Such a measure could help preserve amateurism, increase graduation rates, and allow universities to retain the most talented athletes for the duration of their eligibility.

8. Prohibit the Punishment of Student-Athletes That Have Not Committed a Violation

It is an injustice to punish student-athletes for actions that they did not commit i.e. taking away a team's post-season eligibility for the inappropriate actions of boosters. Such punishment has significant negative impacts on the short college experience of many student-athletes. Alternative forms of punishment are available and should be utilized to allow an adequate policing of the rules.

9. Guarantee That Student-Athletes Are Granted an Athletic Release from Their University If They Wish to Transfer Schools

Schools should not have the power to refuse to release student-athletes that choose to transfer. The NCAA currently gives universities tyrannical power in determining whether or not to allow student-athletes to retain athletic eligibility after transferring. This contradicts the principle of sportsmanship that the NCAA claims to uphold.

10. Allow Student-Athletes of All Sports the Ability to Transfer Schools One Time Without Punishment

Student-athletes that participate in football, basketball, and hockey should not be denied the one-time no-penalty transfer option that is afforded to student-athletes of other sports. Such a policy is coercive and discriminatory. All student-athletes should have this freedom to ensure that they realize their academic, social, and athletic pursuits.

12

College Athletes Should Be Allowed to Unionize

Paul D. Staudohar and Barry Zepel

Paul D. Staudohar is a professor of business at California State University and is the author or editor of 19 books. Barry Zepel has over 20 years of experience as a sportswriter and as a sports information director for many colleges and universities.

College athletes should be considered employees rather than students because their first duty is to play sports for the university, ahead of obtaining an education. They would benefit from being able to unionize, but cannot because they are not paid a wage. College athletes should be allowed to unionize and receive a wage so that they can look out for their interests because the universities, athletic departments, and coaches are not.

Are football and basketball players at Division I-A schools amateurs or professionals? The answer is complicated since categorical notions have changed over time, making for an ideological rather than historical assertion. We know that top college athletes have a full-time commitment to their sport; they function in an organization with emphasis on economic goals; they "work" for bosses (coaches, tutors); and they are contracted to play for a particular team. Athletes receive compensation for tuition and books, housing in collegiate facilities, and sometimes financial assistance from boosters. Their main goal is to participate in sports, not to receive

Paul D. Staudohar and Barry Zeppel, *Economics of College Sports*, Westport, CT: Praeger Publishers, 2004.

an education. There is currently a movement to unionize college athletes, by the United Steelworkers of America, which if successful would be another indication of professionalism. On the other hand, there is no direct payment to athletes in the form of a wage, and an athlete's outside earnings are limited to $2,000 per year.

The purpose of big-time college sports has little if anything to do with the educational mission of the schools. The purpose is to provide entertainment for students, alumni, boosters, and the public-at-large through live game and televised viewing. Elite athletes in top-level programs are ostensibly students, but they are not recruited for academic reasons. Their "scholarships" are based on their playing skills and entertainment value, not on academic capability.

The Basic Problem

There is no doubt that sports are a valuable part of students' campus life, whether playing intramural games or attending sports events for entertainment. However, overemphasis on the big-time sports of football and basketball, especially at the 115 Division I-A schools, has created a monster that, not interested in academic study, would have an alternative route to professional careers. . . .

The large amounts of money paid to the NCAA and universities for big-time basketball and football result mainly from the entertainment value of watching these sports on television. While the athletes participating in these shows receive various forms of compensation, they do not receive a wage. Limited as to how much outside income they can earn, it is not surprising that some of these athletes feel that they are being exploited because they bring in far greater revenues to their schools than the cost of the benefits they receive. The Collegiate Athletes Coalition (the organization supported by the Steelworkers Union) is trying to improve conditions for athletes in Division I men's football and basketball. . . .

The organization of players may be a good idea if it provides a more equitable distribution of money to athletes. Although supported by the Steelworkers, the players' group is not a union as such. According to the National Labor Relations Act, rights to unionize exist only for "employees," and under their current status, college athletes would not be considered employees because they do not receive a wage.

For most athletes, successful educational pursuit would have to wait until their playing days were over.

Time to Change

But perhaps it is time to change the nature of big-time athletic programs in a radical restructuring. Athletes could have a real union and be paid a wage for their services. This would get rid of the hypocrisy of the "student athlete" at schools with corrupt programs and provide honest for-pay entertainment. If such a change were enacted, programs would become self-supporting and not subsidized by public funds. Big-time college sports programs would function as a minor league feeder system to the NFL, NBA, and other major leagues. They would continue to provide entertainment, but as professionals not operating under the guise of amateurism.

If athletes playing for universities under these revised programs want to pursue academic studies, they could do so. But they would have to compete in admissions fairly, pursue authentic curricula with real scholarly content, and be treated and judged just like other students. For most athletes, successful educational pursuit would have to wait until their playing days were over.

13

College Athletes Should Not Be Allowed to Unionize

Dr. Thomas K. Hearn Jr.

Dr. Thomas K. Hearn Jr. was president of Wake Forest University for 22 years before retiring in 2005 to become chair of the Knight Commission, an organization that seeks reforms in college sports.

The Knight Commission on Intercollegiate Athletics was formed in 1989 to study a growing pattern of abuses in college sports. The group issued a report and recommendations in 1990. Some of those recommendations have been followed and the situation has improved in many ways, but there is still much that needs to be done. Part of the problem is that the expense of running a premier sports program keeps going up. Some have suggested that, in this big money environment, athletes should enjoy more economic benefits. One way to do this would be to allow college athletes to form a coalition or union to collectively bargain for their rights. This is a bad idea because it would bring an end to the current system of college athletics and result in the denial of opportunities to many student-athletes. Such a move would also run counter to the academic mission of the universities.

In response to the growing pattern of abuses in college sports during the 1980s, the Knight Foundation, under the leadership of its president, Creed Black, created the Knight Commission on Intercollegiate Athletics in 1989. The Commission

Dr. Thomas K. Hearn Jr., "The Culture of Sport and the Future of Intercollegiate Athletics: Address to the Association of Governing Boards, Boston, MA," www.wfu.edu, April 22, 2002. Reproduced by permission.

was chaired by two of America's most distinguished university presidents, William Friday of North Carolina and Theodore Hesburgh of Notre Dame.

After extensive hearings and deliberations, the Knight Commission's first report, Keeping Faith with the Student-Athlete, recommended reforms reflecting four fundamental principles. First was presidential control. Athletic departments, conferences, and the NCAA [National Collegiate Athletic Association] itself were variously governed and presidential authority was often mitigated. The NCAA, in particular, was an enormously complex and decentralized body and was not under the direct governing authority of presidents. Second, the principle of academic integrity aimed to prevent the widespread exploitation of student-athletes, who often were admitted without adequate preparation for college and kept eligible in a cafeteria assortment of courses that had scant educational purpose or outcome. Third was the principle of financial integrity. It was not uncommon in those not-so-distant days for athletic fund-raising by boosters to take place outside the university. These funds were collected and distributed occasionally without appropriate safeguards and without university control. Fourth, the Commission recommended a peer certification program for athletic departments, reflecting the accreditation procedures and processes that are established mechanisms of quality control in higher education.

Measures reflecting these principles were, in various degrees and guises, adopted by the NCAA. Most significantly, the NCAA came under the governance of a presidential board of directors. As a general outcome, the Knight Commission brought renewed attention to the areas of conflict between the athletic program and the academic mission of the universities of America. That conflict itself, however, was far from resolved.

The Knight Commission Reconvened

In the year 2000, the Knight Foundation decided to assess the status of intercollegiate athletics a decade after publication of its first report. Once again, with the leadership of Presidents Friday and Hesburgh, supported now by Hodding Carter as president of the foundation, a restructured Knight Commission was convened. Its report, A Call to Action, was released in June 2001.

In some respects the system of intercollegiate athletics has never been stronger. In most of our institutions, most sports programs function appropriately. In the effort to diversify our student populations—ethnically, socio-economically, and internationally—the contribution rendered by athletics is substantial. The doors to academic and athletic competition are opening to women with all the attendant positive results.

However, what our study found about the situation of football and men's—and to some extent women's—basketball, was disturbing. The circumstance of these major "revenue" sports in the major programs poses a growing threat to the entire system of intercollegiate athletics. The status of these major programs determines the welfare and outlook for the entire athletic enterprise.

The "Premier" Sports

This threat has to do with the position of these so-called "premier" sports as part of a continuing and dramatic revolution in the culture of sport in America. Historically, the culture of sport in the nation was defined by local community organizations—schools, summer and church leagues, and the YMCA and the YWCA. Across the nation, these sponsors uniformly regarded sport as an educational and developmental undertaking. The values of fitness, teamwork, and fair play were such that sport was universally regarded as a metaphor for moral endeavor. Athletics as an integral element of learning and personal development was axiomatic. Given this conception, athletics is appropriate to the university as a place of learning, the university being the culmination of this community-based athletic culture.

This change in the culture of sport is destructive of the aims of athletics as part of the mission of the university.

Recent decades, however, have brought a profound revolution in this view of athletics. It now seems quaint and naive. The culture of sport today is defined by professional teams, which are part of the media and entertainment industry. In this professional context, games are played, not for love or for learning, but for money, fame, and stardom. The games that professionals play are not, in the primary sense, games at all, but businesses that operate according to the inexorable laws of the marketplace. Sport as learning and as moral education has no foundation in this setting.

Television is the primary agent of this cultural transformation. What television covers, it transforms to its own requirements. For example, how simpleminded we were to believe—as once we did—that television would enhance democratic political culture. Quite the reverse: television transformed our political system to the requirements of the entertainment ethos. Political conventions are now television shows, and politicians are increasingly television and media personalities. Political discourse is packaged in thirty-second sound bites for the evening news.

This change in the culture of sport is destructive of the aims of athletics as part of the mission of the university. Our athletic programs are increasingly regarded by players, coaches, the media, and our fans as part of the entertainment culture. Our teams wear collegiate colors and insignia, but the ethos of major programs is increasingly that of professional franchises. Therein lies the peril for the present and future of collegiate sports.

The Present Circumstance

The implications of this cultural change are everywhere evident in major athletic programs. Let us examine briefly what this cultural change has wrought.

Despite our earlier efforts, graduation rates in the revenue sports are languishing. The most recent NCAA graduation rate report reveals that 51% of Division I-A football players and 32% of men's basketball players earned degrees. These are full-time students who receive four to five academic years of full scholarship support, plus summer sessions if necessary. By any measure, these rates reflect our lack of academic resolve.

The ethical heart of the matter is: Are we providing student-athletes the educational opportunity for which the university exists? We might reconcile ourselves to the excesses of recruitment and commercialism if, as an outcome, students were being educated. If we fail in this regard, however, the enterprise loses its rationale as a university undertaking.

Graduation rates are not the best or only measure of our academic effort. The way these rates are calculated by federal regulation is flawed. A student-athlete who transfers in good standing and graduates on time still counts as a non-graduate for the school transferred from. Graduation numbers are not reported until six years after the date of the entering class, and thus do not provide adequate information about current academic standing.

But whatever indices we use, poor academic outcomes reflect this changed culture. Wake Forest's legendary basketball coach Bones McKinney remarked that he never told a student to go to class or get a degree. "Why else would they be here?" he asked. "They didn't need me to tell them to do what they came to do." That is the message of a bygone coach and a bygone era.

Some coaches rightly conclude that their career aspirations depend on winning, and winning alone, and feel no career motivation to support the academic aspirations of their players. It is wrong to blame the coaches. We hire and reward them. But so-called "power coaches" are media stars oftentimes beyond the reach of presidents and boards. A chancellor remarked to me about such a coach: "It is fortunate that he cares about education. If he didn't, there would be nothing I could do about it."

The Student Perspective

From the student perspective, a growing number of athletes have no interest in education. Their goal is to play as a professional, and they are in school only out of necessity. The disconnect between their personal interest and the aims of the university is manifest in academic failure and behavioral problems that make the papers with alarming regularity.

These adolescent dreams of professional fame and wealth, of course, are deceptive and cruel, akin to those of impoverished families who believe their future opportunity dictates buying lottery tickets. A tiny fraction of Division I football and basketball players will be drafted by the professionals, and fewer yet will ever make a team. A college education is, in fact, what these young people need as an avenue to productive and useful lives—especially those from disadvantaged backgrounds. The entertainment culture, though, mitigates against the appropriate alignment of youthful aspirations and needs.

[I]n the "play for pay" culture of professional athletics, a free education is often not a valued commodity.

Perhaps the most evident outcome of this new culture is an unsustainable rise in athletic spending—what Cedric Dempsey has called the "athletic arms race." In the pursuit of successful franchises, investments are being made in facilities, salaries, and programs at a rate that is unsustainable at best, suicidal at worst.

Popular opinion is, of course, that colleges make millions on athletics. The problem is that the millions we make, we spend, and we spend yet more. According to the most recent reports, just 48 of the 320 schools in Division I operate in the black. The average deficit for the rest is $3 million annually. If the full cost of athletic facilities—including construction and operation—were assessed fully to the athletic department, I suspect that no athletic program in the nation would be solvent.

Coaching salaries are another glaring indication of the spread of the professional outlook to our campuses. Football and basketball salaries routinely now surpass the million-dollar mark. Why? The professions of professional and major college coaching have merged. When coaches migrate seamlessly from the professionals to the collegiate ranks and back, they come and go bringing an outlook about the job along with escalating salaries.

The rising demand to pay college players reflects not only the growing influence of the professional ideal—athletes play for money—but also the lack of regard for the value of education. Given the lifelong earning differential between high school and college graduates, an education should be the most valuable "payment" a student-athlete could receive. But in the "play for pay" culture of professional athletics, a free education is often not a valued commodity.

A Union Would Bring Calamity

If the coalition/union that is attempting to organize student-athletes in California is successful—I am told we cannot discount that prospect—the outcome will be fiscal calamity. Indeed, the success of this coalition would possibly bring the end of intercollegiate athletics as we have known and loved it. The ironic result would be the closing of doors of opportunity for future student-athletes, defeating the purposes the organizers claim to serve.

There seems to be no comprehensive national solution to this looming financial problem. Efforts to limit expenses or salaries through NCAA or other mechanisms are likely to run afoul of anti-trust and other regulations. This crisis can only be averted through the responsible efforts of boards and presidents on your campus and mine.

Our instinct, however, in the face of rising expenses is to do whatever we can to enhance revenue. The resulting spiral of escalating costs chasing escalating revenues leads to abuses of every sort.

I, for one, am not optimistic that we have the resolve to tame this fiscal dragon. Financial excesses, however, have a way of self-correcting. When state legislators or trustees find themselves facing fiscal shortfalls—as we see across the nation—their willingness to subsidize sports enterprises at the expense of academic programs will be tested. That test may come soon.

The Decline of Sportsmanship

Another casualty of the professional ethic is the decline in sportsmanship and rising levels of confrontation between and among players, coaches and fans. Years ago, my son played small-town tennis tournaments when John McEnroe burst on the scene. The next thing we knew, little boys were having on-court tantrums and shouting obscenities for all the world to hear.

This same degrading process is still at work in athletic programs from the youth leagues on up. In the world of professional athletics, the ideal of conformity to standards of personal conduct—any belief in the moral purpose of sport—has no relevance. Fists and Elbows Fly More Frequently heralded a recent headline in *The New York Times* about the NBA season. Taunting and trash-talking has spread from the fields and courts to the stands, and the conduct of our fans forcefully reminds us that "fan" is short for "fanatic."

Sportsmanship could, of course, be supported by the rigorous enforcement of game officials, but the professional culture militates against it. Despite presidential efforts in the ACC [Atlantic Coast Conference] to have basketball officials call technical fouls on players and benches for obscene language, we have not been able to eliminate that conduct. Several episodes involving coaches and players this year required later action by our Commissioner when forceful action was not taken by the officials at the time.

Systems of Governance

The fragmented systems of governance and control over intercollegiate athletics make our programs vulnerable. Colleges and universities are good-to-outstanding managers of the teaching and learning process. We understand what goes on in the classroom, the laboratory, and the library. But in the business that athletics has become, we are often not adequate to the task. The allure of athletic fame and money tempts us, and we often lack the capacity or the resolve to confront powerful athletic interests.

Conferences exercise a wide range of control over our programs, but they often reflect the desire of member institutions to enhance visibility and revenue.

The NCAA receives more than its share of criticism for the regulatory morass we have created. However, it is the organized reflection of our own collective will. Competition generates a climate of distrust reflected in the arcane and complicated rules about recruitment and student-athlete benefits. These rules are much complained of, yet they grow directly from the ethos of competition. The NCAA is divided along every fault—by individual sport, by revenue and non-revenue sport, by big schools and small schools, by women's issues, minority issues, and every other imaginable interest group. In such a setting, it is virtually impossible to reach policy conclusions that are other than a collection of compromises.

The general outcome is that we do not have systems of governance over intercollegiate athletics that are comprehensive or uniform. In the absence of such mechanisms, various internal and external forces are exerted that do not support alignment with our academic mission. . . .

Our Opportunity—And Our Responsibility

Student-athletes arrive on our campuses possessing remarkable gifts. They have developed early in life a passion that demands the fullest measure of life's supreme requirements—dedication, self-sacrifice and commitment to excellence. They have risen above the passivity and apathy that can accompany adolescence in America. Their youthful passion may be sport, but history reveals that games are avenues to lives of service and achievement in other fields of endeavor.

It is our opportunity—and our responsibility—to see that in intercollegiate athletics this passion for play becomes attached to the other callings of life—career, service, and citizenship. We must not fail these young people of such talent and promise.

The boardrooms and presidential and faculty offices of America are filled with men and women of supreme intelligence and good will. There is no issue affecting the future of intercollegiate athletics that we cannot, with common resolve, set right. I urge you to make this resolution our common purpose.

Organizations to Contact

The editors have compiled the following list of organizations concerned with the issues debated in this book. The descriptions are derived from materials provided by the organizations. All have publications or information available for interested readers. The list was compiled on the date of publication of the present volume; the information provided here may change. Be aware that many organizations take several weeks or longer to respond to inquiries, so allow as much time as possible.

America's Athletes with Disabilities
8630 Fenton Street, Suite 920, Silver Spring, MD   20910
(800) 238-7632 • fax: (301) 589-9052
Web site: www.americasathletes.org

America's Athletes with Disabilities 21⁰ Century Mission is to initiate, stimulate, and promote the overall growth and development of sports, recreation, leisure, health, and fitness activities for persons with physical disabilities.

Center for the Study of Sport in Society
Northeastern University, Boston, MA   02115
(617) 373-4025 • fax: (617) 373-4566
Web site: www.sportinsociety.org

The Center is a social justice organization that uses sport to create social change by working locally, nationally, and internationally to promote physical activity, health, violence prevention, and diversity among young people, adults, and college and professional athletes.

Coalition of Intercollegiate Athletics
2007 Co-Chair Professor Nathan Tublitz, Eugene, OR   97403
(541) 346-4510
e-mail: virginia.l.shepherd@vanderbilt.edu
Web site: www.neuro.uoregon.edu/~tublitz/COIA/index.html

The Coalition of Intercollegiate Athletics (COIA) was formed in 2002 and is an alliance of faculty senates from 55 Division I-A universities. The independent organization promotes comprehensive reform of intercollegiate athletics.

The Drake Group
e-mail: info@thedrakegroup.org
Web site: http://thedrakegroup.org

The mission of the Drake Group is to help college faculty and staff to defend academic integrity in the face of the burgeoning college sport industry. The Drake Group lobbies for proposals that ensure quality education for college athletes, supports faculty whose job security is threatened for defending academic standards, and provides information on current issues involving sports and higher education.

Gay & Lesbian Athletics Foundation
P.O. Box 425034, Cambridge, MA   02142
(617) 588-0600 • fax: (617) 588-0600
e-mail: info@glaf.org
Web site: www.glaf.org

The Gay & Lesbian Athletics Foundation (GLAF) promotes acceptance and visibility of the gay, lesbian, bisexual, and transgendered athletics community through education, mentoring, training, support networks, promotion of positive role models and healthy lifestyles, and advocating for inclusion, recognition, understanding, and respect.

Knight Commission on Intercollegiate Athletics
Executive Director, Amy Perko
(910) 864-5782
Web site: www.knightcommission.org

Formed in 1989, the Knight Commission on Intercollegiate Athletics has sought to be an agent of change in trying to reconnect college sports with the educational mission of

America's colleges and universities. The Commission also encourages faculty members at colleges to become involved in issues involving athletics.

National College Players Association
Web site: www.cacnow.org

The National College Players Association (NCPA), formerly known as the College Athletes Coalition, was formed in 2001 by a group of former UCLA football players. The group seeks to be a voice for the interests of college athletes. The group claims to have pressured the NCAA into making a number of reforms that benefit college athletes.

National Collegiate Athletic Association
700 W. Washington Street, Indianapolis, IN   46206-6222
(317) 917-6222 • fax: (317) 917-6888
Web site: www.ncaa.org

The National Collegiate Athletic Association (NCAA) is a voluntary organization through which U.S. colleges and universities govern their athletic programs. Over 1,000 academic institutions are members of the NCAA. The NCAA's stated "Core Purpose" is to, among other things, "integrate intercollegiate athletics into higher education so that the educational experience of the student-athlete is paramount."

National Institute for Sports Reform
P.O. Box 128, Selkirk, NY   12158
fax: (518) 439-7284
e-mail: director@nisr.org
Web site: www.nisr.org

One of the National Institute for Sports Reform's several missions is to "end the exploitation and abuse of youth, scholastic, amateur, and collegiate athletes." The organization seeks to reform a "runaway sports culture" by studying and advocating sports reforms at the pre-professional level.

National Student Athletes' Rights Movement

2006 Kasold, Lawrence, Kansas 66047
fax: (785) 842-0670
e-mail: info@studentathletesrights.org
Web site: www.studentathletesrights.org

The National Student Athletes' Rights Movement was founded in 2002 by a former University of Kansas track and field coach. It seeks to encourage debates in public forums on issues of intercollegiate athletics as well as focusing public attention on the need for changes to help protect the welfare of student-athletes.

Women's Sports Foundation

Eisenhower Park, East Meadow, NY 11554
(800) 227-3988 • fax: (516) 542-4716
e-mail: info@womenssportsfoundation.org
Web site: www.womenssportsfoundation.org

The mission of the Women's Sports Foundation is to advance the lives of girls and women through sport and physical activity.

Bibliography

Books

Eric Anderson
In the Game: Gay Athletes and the Cult of Masculinity. Albany, NY: State University of New York, 2005.

Charles Barkley
I May Be Wrong, But I Doubt It. Ed. Michael Wilbon, New York: Random House, 2002.

William G. Bowen and Sarah A. Levin
Reclaiming the Game: College Sports and Educational Values. Princeton, NJ: Princeton University Press, 2003.

Todd Boyd
Young, Black, Rich, and Famous: The Rise of the NBA, the Hip Hop Invasion, and the Transformation of American Culture. New York: Doubleday, 2003.

Joseph N. Crowley
In the Arena: The NCAA's First Century. Indianapolis, IN: National Collegiate Athletic Association, 2006.

D. Stanley Eitzen
Fair and Foul: Beyond the Myths and Paradoxes of Sport. Lanham, MD: Rowman & Littlefield Publishers, 2003.

John Feinstein
Last Dance: Behind the Scenes at the Final Four. New York: Little Brown, 2006.

John Fizel and Rodney Fort, eds.
Economics of College Sports. Westport, CT: Praeger, 2004.

Jessica Gavora	*Tilting the Playing Field: Schools, Sports, Sex, and Title IX*. San Francisco: Encounter Books, 2002.
John R. Gerdy	*Air Ball: American Education's Failed Experiment With Elite Athletics*. Jackson, MS: University of Mississippi Press, 2006.
Pamela Grundy and Susan Shackelford	*Shattering The Glass: The Remarkable History of Women's Basketball*. New York: New Press, 2005.
Carl E. James	*Race in Play: Understanding the Socio-Cultural Worlds of Student-Athletes*. Toronto: Canadian Scholars' Press, 2005.
Michael Lewis	*The Blind Side: Evolution of a Game*. New York: W.W. Norton & Company, 2006.
Chris Lincoln	*Playing the Game: Inside Athletic Recruiting in the Ivy League*. White River Junction, VT: Nomad Press, 2004.
Cynthia Lee A. Pemberton	*More Than a Game: One Woman's Fight For Gender Equity in Sport*. Boston: Northeastern University Press, 2002.
Christopher Russo with Allen St. John	*The Mad Dog 100: The Greatest Sports Arguments of All Time*. New York: Doubleday, 2003.
Kenneth L. Shropshire and Timothy Davis	*The Business of Sports Agents*. Philadelphia: University of Pennsylvania Press, 2002.

James L. Shulman and William G. Bowen	*The Game of Life: College Sports and Educational Values*. Princeton, NJ: Princeton University Press, 2005.
Welch Suggs	*A Place on the Team: The Triumph and Tragedy of Title IX*. Princeton, NJ: Princeton University Press, 2005.
Ying Wushanley	*Playing Nice and Losing: The Struggle For Control of Women's Intercollegiate Athletics, 1960–2000*. Syracuse, NY: Syracuse University Press, 2004.

Periodicals

Shelly Anderson	"Anderson: NCAA Rules Too Thorny for Bloom," *Pittsburgh Post-Gazette*, October 13, 2005.
Dwayne Ballen	"An Incentive Clause for College Athletes?," *American Public Media: Marketplace*, January 8, 2007. http://marketplace.publicradio.org.
Jeff Barker	"Congressman Thinks Colleges Should Pay Athletes," *Baltimore Sun*, May 2, 2007.
Scott Bordow	"Look, College Athletes Already Get Paid," *East Valley Tribune* (Mesa, AZ), January 2, 2003.
Marcia Chambers	"Colleges; Brand Endorses More Aid To Athletes," *New York Times*, September 18, 2003.

Dan Daly   "At Waffle House, Menu Choices Not Final," *Washington Times*, June 7, 2007.

Frank Deford   "Pay Dirt: College Athletes Deserve Same Rights As Other Students," *SI.com*, May 7, 2003. http://sportsillustrated.cnn.com.

Michael J. Diacin, Janet B. Parks, and Pamela C. Allison   "Voices of Male Athletes on Drug Use, Drug Testing, and the Existing Order in Intercollegiate Athletics," *Journal of Sport Behavior*, vol. 26, no. 1, March 2003.

David Enders   "Football Players Discussed Joining Players' Association," *Michigan Daily*, April 10, 2002.

Patrick Finley   "UA Football Penalized for Academic Woes," *Arizona Daily Star*, May 3, 2007.

Teddy Greenstein   "ESPN Views Play-for-Pay Arguments," *Chicago Tribune*, March 15, 2005.

Steve Hanway   "Pay for Play a Bad Idea," *Big Red Network*, January 19, 2007. http://bigrednetwork.com.

Ali Hasnain   "Should College Athletes Be Paid Wages?" *The Daily Utah Chronicle*, September 12, 2003.

Debbie Lazorik   "Why Integrate Athletics Back into Campus Life?" *Women in Higher Education*, vol. 15, no. 12, December 2006.

Mike Lopresti   "Commentary: Don't Pay College
                       Football Athletes to Play," *Gannett
                       News Service*, February 13, 2003.

John Maher   "Longhorns Get No NCAA Penalties
                       for Academics," *Austin American-
                       Statesman*, May 3, 2007.

Pete Pelegrin   "Penalties Are No Surprise," *Miami
                       Herald*, May 3, 2007.

Selena Roberts   "The Wal-Mart Of College Sports,"
                       New York Times, June 3, 2007.

Doug Smock   "Pay for Play? Get Real," *Charleston
                       Gazette*, February 12, 2007.

Kevin Tatum   "Do the Homework, Then You Can
                       Play: Temple Has a New Way to Keep
                       Student-Athletes Eligible, and, More
                       Important, Educated," *Philadelphia
                       Inquirer*, November 10, 2006.

Eddie Timanus   "Academic Sanctions to Hit 65
                       Schools," *USA Today*, March 2, 2006.

Kelly Whiteside   "College Athletes Want Cut of Ac-
                       tion," *USA Today*, August 31, 2004.

Lya Wodraska   "Poor Academics Cost Weber Foot-
                       ball Scholarships," *Salt Lake Tribune*,
                       May 3, 2007.

Brad Wolverton   "Athletics Participation Prevents
                       Many Players From Choosing Majors
                       They Want," *Chronicle of Higher Edu-
                       cation*, vol. 53, no. 20, January 19,
                       2007.

Index